RELIGION

CONCEPT BOOKS

General Editor: Alan Harris

RELIGION

JOHN WILSON

 HEINEMANN EDUCATIONAL BOOKS
LONDON

Heinemann Educational Books Ltd
LONDON EDINBURGH MELBOURNE TORONTO
AUCKLAND JOHANNESBURG SINGAPORE
IBADAN NAIROBI HONG KONG NEW DELHI
KUALA LUMPUR

ISBN 0 435 46194 X

Published in Great Britain by
Heinemann Educational Books Ltd
48 Charles Street, London W1X 8AH
Printed in Great Britain by
Cox & Wyman Ltd
London, Reading and Fakenham

Preface

WHATEVER DISAGREEMENTS there may be about the nature of religion and religious education, everyone will agree that there is a good deal of confusion in this area. Given such a situation – and it is one which perhaps applies particularly to young people – there is, I think, only one clear way forwards and that is to invite the reader to investigate this area for himself, rather than handing him some doctrinaire (and possibly wrong) view on a plate.

This is the course which I have tried to adopt in this book. Part I consists essentially of a philosophical inquiry into the concept of religion: for unless we make up our minds about this first, we shall not be able to make much progress. Some of the views here considered appear also in my *Education in Religion and the Emotions*,[1] but my purpose has not been to try to bully the reader into accepting any particular doctrine about the nature of religion – that would not be proper philosophical inquiry at all, but a rather rarefied kind of indoctrination. I have tried only to expose certain prejudices and lay certain considerations before the reader.

In Part II I have tried, by various comparative methods, to give something of the inner 'stuff' of religion: in particular some understanding of the human needs and emotions with which it is connected. It will be appreciated that, in so small a space, I have not been able to give detailed summaries or 'factual' accounts of the various religions of the world. Nor do I think this to be desirable in the first instance. If the reader can gain some understanding of *what religion is about*, an understanding broadened and supported by particular instances, he will be able to study aspects of

[1] Heinemann Educational Books (1971).

different religions for himself. I have added a short bibliography
which he may find helpful here.

J.B.W.

Oxford 1972

Contents

one

What Religion is Not

SOMEONE TALKING about religion is supposed to have added: 'When I say "religion", of course I mean the Christian religion: and by the Christian religion of course I mean the Church of England'. This remark is usually quoted with a smile, because the man seems so obviously biased or prejudiced. But a lot of this book will be an attempt to escape from this bias and prejudice, which is far more deeply rooted than most of us like to think.

Note first that there are *two kinds* of prejudice here. (a) We can have prejudices about whether a particular religion, or a particular sect within that religion (like the Church of England), is a good thing, or true, or right, or better than any other: just as we might be prejudiced in favour of the Labour or the Conservative Party, or the Marxists, or some other political creed. But much more important (b) we may be prejudiced about *what religion is*, what the word 'religion' means. This is a very different and more fundamental kind of mistake. It would be rather like saying 'By "politics" of course I mean socialist politics, and by "socialist politics" of course I mean the policies of the Labour Party'. This is much worse than (a) just thinking that the policies of the Labour Party are right: it is (b) thinking that nothing counts as 'politics' except Labour Party policies.

Clearly we shall not be in any position to consider what religions or religious sects are true, or right, or sensible, if we start off with a false view about what religion is. So in Part I of this book we shall be considering this prior question. It is a very difficult question; in particular, people find it hard to answer because (like the man quoted above) most of us just *take it for granted* that 'religion' means the kind of religion we ourselves are used to. We easily fall victims to our own particular environment and culture, and assume that the only things that count are those we are familiar with. Thus to many people in this country 'religion' and 'Christinaity' are often used to mean more or less the same thing (e.g. when there are arguments about 'religious education'): yet we know quite well, when we stop to think, that there are plenty of other religions.

But this is only one obvious example of a prejudice about what 'religion' is. What we need is a list of human activities or types of thinking which are apt to be taken as typically 'religious', when in fact they are not; so that we can get clear about our possible prejudices and go on to consider what religion really is. There are a great many such activities and types of thinking, and I shall list only the most important and those most likely to be wrongly taken as essentially 'religious'. Of course many of these activities may have gone on *under the name of particular religions*, but that is not our concern: what we are interested in is the core or essence of anything that could count as a religion.

1. *Not just Christianity or the 'higher' religions*
Only a very careless or prejudiced person would talk as if 'religion' meant 'Christianity'; but more people are apt to talk as if religion was confined to what are sometimes (again with prejudice) called the 'higher' religions. These are the monotheistic religions, and are commonly thought to be morally superior: among them are Christianity, Buddhism, the Jewish faith, Mohammedanism and perhaps certain forms of Hinduism. But of course there are plenty of other religions which are not like these, yet are still perfectly good cases of religion: the polytheistic religion of the ancient Greeks and Romans, the nature-worship common to many primitive peoples, and so on. Here we can see the essence of our prejudice at work: because we (or some of us) *approve* more of these 'higher religions', we tacitly refuse to count the others as religion at all. This is an obvious cheat.

2. *Not just morals*
One thing that has certainly been often – perhaps almost always –

associated with religion is some kind of moral code, set of values, way of life, rules or standards of behaviour, etc.: as for instance the Ten Commandments, or the moral sayings of Jesus, in the case of Christianity. So it is easy to talk as if religion just *was* a set of moral principles, perhaps dressed up in rather grand language. Thus we might say 'All men are brothers', or 'God our Father wants us all to love each other': and this might look like no more than a piece of moral advice.

Of course there are connections between religion and morality: but they are not the same thing. We can see this most easily by looking at the ancient Greek religion, or the religion of the Norsemen. Here there are undoubtedly gods, powerful and awesome, to be worshipped in various ways. But the Greeks and the Norsemen did not always think that their gods were *good* or *morally authoritative*. Some of the gods were evil; many more were neither good nor bad, but just powerful. In Euripides' play *Hippolytus* the hero is under the influence of two goddesses: Aphrodite (standing for sexual passion) and Artemis (standing for chastity or purity). It is clear in the play that both these are powerful goddesses, and the hero comes to grief through disregarding – not worshipping – Aphrodite: but there is no question of one or the other of them being *morally good*.

It is often tempting, particularly for people who are uncertain about the point of religion, to assume that religion is just about morals: about what we ought to do. A lot of the interest in the Christian church concerns what attitude the church ought to take to contemporary problems: to war, poverty, racial prejudice, and so forth. But this is a mistake. Religions and churches must, somehow, be distinct from political parties or social welfare workers: there must be something specific which *priests* and *religion* are concerned with, which is different from what anyone else who has an interest in morals and politics and society is concerned with.

3. *Not magic or science*

Another thing has also often been part of particular religions, and closely associated with religion in general: and that is the whole area of *explaining* physical events and phenomena, and effecting changes in the physical world. Christians, for instance, say such things as 'God made the world', 'Jesus turned the water into wine', 'St Paul healed the sick'; and in other religions gods are supposed to send down fire from heaven, strike people with thunderbolts, make the crops grow or the rain fall, and so forth. They are supposed to *perform* in the physical world in some way or other.

This cannot be at the heart of religion, because it comes under another category: a category which nowadays we call 'science', and which in the past might have been called 'magic' or 'alchemy'. We know perfectly well that, if we want to explain things in the physical world or alter what happens, we have to go in for science: we have to find out by experiment and careful observation what happens and why it happens. To say things like 'God did it', or 'It's a miracle' is to throw in the sponge: such remarks don't help, because they don't explain anything or add to our knowledge of nature.

Note that, even if it were proved that there was some super-being in outer space, or in some unimaginable fourth dimension, thus still would not be anything to do with *religion*. In some science-fiction stories the author sometimes imagines the existence of such a super-being: an immensely powerful creature from another galaxy who has started our world off as an experiment, for instance. This might be true: but what has it got to do with *religion*? Insofar as it just adds to our knowledge of the universe, it is no more than a piece of science: a very important piece, no doubt, but still just science.

4. Not 'a spiritual state of mind' or 'experience'

Under this heading I want to include a lot of things that people have sometimes *got out of* religion, or used religion *for*. For instance, many people claim to have had some 'religious experience': a feeling that there was an 'outside power' with whom they were in contact, some kind of 'vision', the hearing of 'voices', a 'meeting with the supernatural', and so on. Other people, sometimes under the influence of drugs, have talked of being 'out of this world', 'in a mystic trance', 'a state of ecstasy', etc. Others again practise some kind of self-discipline, and by fasting or praying or meditation try to achieve a certain 'spiritual state of mind'.

It is clear that this does not necessarily have anything to do with religion: first, because there are plenty of people who 'have a religion' without having or even talking about such 'experiences'; and secondly, because there are plenty of people who have these 'experiences' and are in these states of mind without 'having a religion'. It is only when such people start to talk about *God*, or imply some kind of *belief*, or *worship*, that we feel at all tempted to connect their states of mind with religion.

What seems to happen is this: if someone *already has* a religion, and then has certain 'other-worldly' experiences, he will probably describe these in religious language. He will talk of 'God', 'angel voices', 'communion with Christ', or in whatever language his religion suggests to him. Other people, on whom the language of a particular religion has a weaker hold, may talk of 'the infinite', 'reality', 'beyond space and time', etc.: others again may simply say that they felt ecstatic, dream-like, carried away, 'out of this world'. Drug-takers or mental patients, for instance, do not necessarily give a religious form to their experiences. There are plenty of people in the modern world who claim to be seeking for some kind of special experience, or 'new life', far removed from the normal experience of existing society (which they find distasteful or horrible): but comparatively few of these would count as having a *religion*.

5. *Not just rituals or organizations*
We might be tempted to think that religion was essentially a matter of some kind of communal or organized ritual: the kind of thing that goes on in a church, or a Buddhist temple, or a Mohammedan mosque. And of course most, perhaps all, religions have had some kind of organization and some kind of common rituals or forms of worship. But the heart of religion does not lie here.

The chief point here is that we would not be able to identify a ritual or an organization as *religious* unless we also knew something *else* about it. People bow down to churches and mosques, but so they do in gymnasiums and palaces. Churches have leaders and rules, but so do political parties and businesses. What makes the difference lies not in what they overtly *do* – not in their physical movements – but in the *intentions* and *beliefs* with which they do it. You can bow down to worship and pray, or bow down to exercise your back-muscles.

We could not describe a ritual or organization as 'religious' without using words like 'creed', 'faith', 'prayer', 'sacrifice', 'worship', and so on. Here again, as in 2 above, we wonder what it is that is *specific* to religion. Just as a 'priest' or 'clergyman' is not primarily to be defined as somebody who gives moral advice, so too he is not primarily somebody who goes through certain rituals, or wears certain clothes, or has a place in an organization.

6. *Not just 'ultimate concern', 'ideals', etc.*

A more popular move nowadays is to say that 'religion' is just what a person's 'ultimate concern' or 'ultimate values' are: what he believes to be important, what sort of picture he has of life as a whole. Some modern Christian theologians[1] have taken this line. But plainly it does not fit 'religion' in general.

First, there are and have been lots of religions which are far more unsophisticated than this. Those who worshipped Zeus or Jehovah or Wotan would not have understood a lot of the modern talk about 'ultimate reality', 'the purpose of life', and so on. They had their god, worshipped him, and took little interest in high-sounding and complicated metaphysics. Indeed most Christians, even today, have a much more simple kind of religion than modern theologians make out: they worship God and Jesus, and have little time for whatever is meant by 'ultimate concern'.

Secondly, this move would force us to say that, in some sense, *everybody* had a religion. For no doubt everybody has some picture of life, some idea of what he takes to be of overriding importance – pleasure, money, the Communist Party, power, or whatever. But we do not, in normal English, count attachment to these 'ultimate concerns' as *religion*. If a person actually *worshipped* money or the Communist Party, we might then begin to think he had a religion: but not till then. Everybody has values, or (if you like) some 'ultimate concern': but not everybody has a religion.

[1] The quickest way of finding out about these is to read John Robinson's *Honest to God*, and take up the references in it to other writers (Bonhoeffer, Tillich, etc.).

7. *Not just history*

Some people, including some Christians, will be tempted to think that religion is a matter of historical fact. 'Christ was born, died for our sins, rose from the dead, healed the sick and so on: that's our religion, and it's true as a matter of history.' But here again, although no doubt many religions *make use of* historical facts (or what are thought to be facts), the essentially 'religious' part of them cannot be a matter of history.

What happened in history is common to everybody: but whether we make a religion out of it depends on something else. For instance, let us suppose that it is not in dispute that a man called Jesus was born at such-and-such a time, spoke certain words, died, came to life again, and so forth. All this is a matter of history: if we are in doubt, we turn to expert historians to advise us. But once we begin talking in a specifically religious way it is no longer a matter of history. Thus if we say 'the *son of God* was born', or '*God gave* Jesus the power to do so-and-so', then non-Christians will at once disagree. They will accept the down-to-earth historical facts, but not the religious description of them – the man Jesus, but not the son of God.

To Christians, the words and deeds of Jesus seem such as to merit such description as 'the son of God'. That is, they seem to merit a certain attitude – roughly, the attitude of *worship*. In the same way, we might all agree about what Mohammed or Hitler or Lenin or some other person did in history: but to one person Hitler seems a demi-god, to be revered and obeyed, whereas to another he seems a raving idiot. History does not dictate our religion to us.

It would be possible to extend this list of things that religion is not, almost indefinitely. But perhaps we can now, at least, begin to see what our real problem is. It is to identify something that religion *is*, in the sense of some function of job or form of life that religion (and nothing else) fulfils. What we have done is to go through a number of functions that we have dismissed as 'not essentially religious', because they are jobs which can be better done by other things, not religion. I shall try to spell this out a bit more clearly.

If you look at the history of some religions, such as Christianity over the last few centuries, you will be struck by the way in which religion seems to be in a state of permanent retreat. In the old days, many Christians seemed to use their religion to do the job which we now think to be better done by science. Christians would dispute the facts of evolution, or claim as 'miracles' events which we now either think did not occur at all, or can explain scientifically. In the same sort of way primitive peoples might believe that their gods 'swallow the moon' during an eclipse. So nowadays most Christians do not use their religion in this way any more: they do not expect God to perform magically in the physical world – they do not have that kind of God. We have science instead.

This, then, is one retreat that religion has made – away from science, which has taken over one of its functions (or what was thought to be one of its functions). So then, perhaps, Christians believed that at least God would help them with their own mental problems, if not in the physical world. Perhaps God can make us less neurotic or unhappy, or even cure us of some diseases by 'faith': or perhaps he can solve our moral problems for us by telling us what is right and wrong. But then, in recent history, more and more people come to see that we have or can develop techniques for solving these problems too – not scientific techniques, but perhaps the technique of psychology, moral philosophy, and so forth. Nowadays we may go to the priest if we are in distress, but we are more likely to go to the psychotherapist.

So then Christianity makes another retreat: God no longer performs in the material world, and now no longer in the mental world either. We have doctors, psychologists, welfare workers, and so forth to do all these jobs for us. What then is left? What is there that religion, and the priests of religion, can do, that other things and other experts cannot do better? As we have seen, if we are interested in science, or morals, or mental health, or history, then we naturally turn to other experts. What is the expertise of religion? What can religious experts tell us that other people cannot?

We shall try and answer this in what follows; but meanwhile

watch out for two prejudices. Those who are by temperament or upbringing opposed to religion are apt to give too quick an answer by replying 'Nothing: religion has no special function or task: it is just a mixture of a lot of other things (science, morals, etc.) which we now know how to do better for ourselves. We have grown out of religion: it was never more than a stop-gap, a crutch to lean on for those who did not have the benefits of science and psychology and other serious ways of dealing with life'. This is a tempting view, if only because a great deal of actual religions in the past *have* been (mostly, at least) a mixture of this kind. But the temptation must be resisted. For (a) not *all* religion in the past has been *only* this; (b) even if it had been, that would not mean that there were not something that could properly be called 'religion' which would be worth doing. (In the same way, a lot of mediaeval 'science' was a muddle of alchemy, astrology, black magic and so on: but nevertheless a proper form of thought, which we now call 'science', emerged from it.)

The other prejudice is to say 'There's nothing special or worth having about religion *in general*, and it's foolish to try to compare "religion" with "science" or other forms of thought. But my *particular* religion is true and important. I don't want to defend, or even investigate, religion in general: but I take my stand on Christianity' (or Buddhism, or Mohammedanism, or whatever the speaker's religion is). The objection to this is that we cannot tell if this particular religion is any good, unless and until we first know what 'religion' is in general. In the same way, if we were comparing one scientific or one moral view with another, trying to work out which (if either) was right, we should have first to get a general idea of what counted as a good scientific or moral view: we should have to understand about science and morals as a whole. At present we do not even know what the speaker *means* when he says that he has a 'religion': if it isn't a set of scientific or historical or moral beliefs, just what *is* it?

I hope at least in this first chapter to have shown something of the *kind* of problem we have to face. Our difficulty – and this is likely to crop up in the reader's mind on all sorts of occasions – is that, because we tend to take sides too quickly, we fail to face the problem at all. Unfortunately this is the case with many past writers on religion. 'Religion is the opium of the people', wrote Marx: the Bible says 'True religion is this: to do justly and to love mercy . . .': Freud says religion is a 'universal neurosis'; and so on. All these people may have something important to say about religion: but they do not help us to see clearly what religion is. They are partisan. And whatever else may be said about religion, it is obviously too important for us to sweep it into the pocket of some prejudice.

two

What Religion Is

RELIGION IS connected to, or made up of, certain kinds of human activities with which we are all familiar: worshipping, adoring, praying, sacrificing, revering and so forth. These activities involve three things: (a) some kind of *emotion*, (b) various *beliefs*, and (c) different sorts of *behaviour*.

Let us start with (a), the emotion. Of course all sorts of emotions come into religion. A person who believed religiously in Jesus or Mohammed might feel love, admiration, respect and so on: he might feel guilty or ashamed if he disobeyed Jesus. But a person who had no religious belief in Jesus or Mohammed might also feel these emotions. What, then, is the difference? Is there some specifically religious emotion which the believer will feel, and the other person – who might be just a friend – will not necessarily feel?

There is such an emotion, and the best word for it in English is 'awe'. The word is not commonly used nowadays, and is often confused with other words which have a different meaning. 'Awe' is not the same as 'fear', or 'respect', or 'wonder'. It is a bit like 'reverence', only stronger: I can revere somebody without necessarily going so far as to be in awe of him. 'Being in awe' means something like 'finding overwhelmingly impressive', 'regarding something or somebody as powerful, majestic, mighty, tremendous'. It does not involve thinking that the object of awe is necessarily *good* (or bad): only that it is something you ought to look up to, feel smaller than, or be impressed by.

It is logically possible to be in awe of anything; but there are certain characteristic objects of awe – usually large, powerful and mysterious things. Small children are naturally, from time to time, in awe of their parents: you may be in awe of the pyramids, a thunderstorm, the star-spangled heavens – or of your boss, your teacher, your king or dictator, your hero, your girl-friend. Or you can be more sophisticated, and be in awe of Nature, or Reason, or the universe, or humanity as a whole: of the marvels of science, or the mysteries of human feelings and emotions.

Turning to (b), the beliefs, we can begin to see that the religious believer must not just *be* in awe, but must also think that the object of his awe is an *appropriate* object, and that it is important for him to keep his feeling of awe alive. For instance, I might find myself feeling awe of Hitler or my boss, but say to myself 'This is silly, Hitler is really just a maniac, and my boss is nothing special: I can't help my feelings at the moment, but I'm not going to endorse them. Hitler and my boss aren't the sort of people I *ought* to feel in awe of.' But a religious believer would think that Jesus, or Mohammed, or whoever, were *worthy recipients* of awe.

Note that this gives us something *specifically* religious, the sort of thing that we were looking for in the last chapter. A specifically religious belief will be a belief that such-and-such or so-and-so is an appropriate object of awe. To be a true Christian, to worship Jesus, is essentially to think that Jesus is a person whom one ought to be in awe of and to worship (not just a great ethical teacher or a nice chap). Of course there will be other sorts of beliefs too – the Christian believes, for instance, that Jesus actually existed, and did such-and-such. But the specifically *religious* belief is that a certain attitude – the attitude of awe and worship – is appropriate. The central features of a religion are found in pronouncements like 'Worthy art thou, O God, to receive honour and power and glory . . .', 'Holy, holy, holy, Lord God Almighty', 'Great is God', and so on.

This brings in (c), the behavioural element. There is a charac-teristic expression of awe: namely, *worship*. A person who believes that awe is appropriate for a certain object, and believes further that this is a very important truth, will want to cherish and foster the appropriate feeling by certain rituals and organizations. He will want to *celebrate* the feeling by singing, dancing, going through certain ritual motions appropriate to it (bowing down, kneeling, etc.), declaring its appropriateness in creeds and psalms and hymns, and so on. This is worship. To worship something is to express one's belief that awe is the appropriate thing to be felt towards it.

This too is specifically religious. A true case of worship is a true case of religion. Certainly we say things like 'He worships money', or 'She worships the ground he walks on', but we are only half-serious. If a person seriously believed that he ought to be in awe of money, and had some kind of ritual whereby he knelt down before dollars or pound notes, raised his hands and said 'O mighty money!', and so forth, then we should say that he had a religion. For this would show that he felt he ought to be in awe of money and worship it (not just that he was very fond of money, which would not be enough for religion).

These are the bare bones of religion; and it is important to understand them before we try to fill them out with flesh. I am claiming that anyone who (in the full sense) worships anything – thinking awe to be appropriate, and 'celebrating' this belief in some organized way – has a religion: and that anyone who does not, does not have a religion. For instance, the question of whether Communism is a religion turns (on this view) on whether Communists just have a way of life, or a moral and political code, or certain historical or scientific beliefs, on the one hand, or whether they actually *worship* anything on the other hand. Thus if there is some tendency for them to bow or kneel before Lenin's tomb, or to say 'O mighty Lenin, you are the greatest thing in the universe!', in a serious way, then we might begin to think that this at least bordered on religion.

In particular religions (as we shall see in Part II), other activities are added to this. Most believers not only worship, but pray and sacrifice to their objects of worship. Often they suppose that these objects will perform magically for them, sending down fire from heaven, or making the crops grow, or averting flood and fire: often they think that they are moral authorities who should be obeyed. Usually they are conceived as *persons*, to whom they should pray, sacrifice, confess and owe allegiance. But none of these additions are *necessary* for the notion of religion. All that is necessary is awe and worship.

I have spoken of 'objects of worship', and you might think that a shorter way of speaking would be just to say 'gods'. One can however be in awe of and worship things without actually *calling* them 'gods', though most religions do have some such word to name their worship-objects. But there are lots of border-line cases, such as the many animals of ancient Egypt who were indeed held 'sacred' (whatever that may mean) or 'holy', without actually being called 'gods'; and they were worshipped in some sense.

What is important here, whether or not we are going to call any worship-object 'a god', is to realize that practically anything can be a worship-object or god. In our culture we are too apt to raise questions like 'Does God exist?', as if that were the only important question for religion. But 'God', in our culture, spelt with a capital G, refers to only *one kind* of god: either the Christian kind, or at any rate the sort of god characteristic of the 'higher' religions like Mohammedanism. There might be other gods but not *this* God. When Greek sceptics asked whether 'the gods' existed, they were talking about something quite different – the Olympian gods (Zeus, Apollo, etc.): and so with other questions raised in other societies. Different cultures have different gods.

We can now see a little more clearly what is involved in asking about 'the existence of God' (or of 'the gods', 'a god', etc.). Of course we can ask about God (god) in a quite non-religious way. If we were historians, we could ask 'What were the gods of the ancient Greeks, the Babylonians, the Egyptians, etc.?', meaning only 'What sort of worship-objects did they have?' We should not here be concerned with whether these gods really existed, or were worth worshipping: we should just be concerned with facts about ancient Greek, Babylonian, etc. culture. But more usually, when we ask whether God or the gods exist, we are interested in *whether there is something worth worshipping*.

Suppose there was some scientific evidence which made us think that our world, or perhaps our whole galaxy, was in fact created by and under the control of some immensely powerful super-being in another galaxy, or in some unimaginable 'fourth dimension'. Then we would dispute the question 'Does this super-being exist?', and parties to the dispute would bring forward various pieces of evidence for or against. But so far this has nothing much to do with *religion*. If there were such a super-being, we should not want to call him (it) 'God' or 'a god' unless we made a further and quite different move: the move of thinking that we ought to be in awe of and *worship* this being. Whether something exists is one question (usually a question for science): whether something *worshipful* exists is quite another.

Elements of religious belief

There are thus two sorts of mistake a religious believer can make. His overall belief in God (or however he describes what he worships) breaks down into two parts:

(a) that there is something (somebody) which has certain characteristics (call them x, y and z);
(b) that x, y and z are worshipful characteristics, so that this thing or person should be worshipped.

For instance, a primitive savage might believe
(a) that there are people (witch-doctors or supernatural spirits) which have certain characteristics (they can heal the sick, and kill men at a distance by magic);
(b) that these characteristics make the people worth worshipping.
Or a Christian might believe
(a) that there was a person (Jesus) who had certain characteristics (able to heal the sick, kind to his friends, willing to lay down his life for others);
(b) that this is the sort of person one ought to worship.

Of course it is not always clear, in the case of actual religious believers, what their precise beliefs are. Thus another Christian might be less impressed by Jesus' kindness and love, and more impressed by his power. His beliefs might be
(a) that there was a person (Jesus) who had certain characteristics (able to turn water into wine, to rise from the dead, to work miracles, etc.);
(b) that this is the sort of person one ought to worship.
Others again might be impressed by Jesus' ethical teaching, the effect he created on his disciples and on the church they founded, his tragic suffering and death, and so forth. And naturally yet others might be impressed by all the features of Jesus' life, or by none of them.

The importance of separating out these two elements of religious belief is this. First, the believer may be mistaken about the *hard facts*. If witch-doctors cannot in fact kill men at a distance by magic: if Jesus was not willing to lay down his life, help his friends, etc. and could not in fact turn water into wine, rise from the dead and so forth: then in all these examples of (a), and all similar examples, the believer is simply mistaken about what is the case. In the extreme case, if Jesus never existed, then the believer could no longer worship a real historical figure – for there was never any such figure. But secondly, he may be mistaken about the *rightness of his attitude* to the facts. Whether or not witch-doctors can kill men at a distance, or Jesus rose from the dead, it is still another question whether we would be *right to worship* such people with such characteristics. You and a Nazi might agree (a) about all the *facts* relating to Hitler: yet (b) you might think that these facts showed Hitler to be the last person one ought to worship, whereas the Nazi might think the opposite.

Of these two elements, (a) and (b), it is (b) which has the most right to be called a specifically *religious* belief – though both are important. The point is that mistakes in (a) are mistakes of fact: historical fact, or scientific fact. They are not mistakes *in religion* though of course they affect particular religions. What is wrong with bad religions, like Baal-worship or Hitler-worship, is not so much that their adherents were incompetent scientists or historians and hence got the facts wrong: it is rather that they attached their emotions and their worship to the *wrong sort of object*.

Sophisticated belief

The distinction between (a) and (b) above is peculiarly important nowadays, when not many people (at least in industrialized countries, where science flourishes) believe naïvely in super-beings who perform magically for our benefit or harm, in the way that the gods in Homer performed – by turning aside spears, causing plagues, sending false dreams and so on. Most people no longer worship a god who sends down fire from heaven in any simple sense: and many people no longer believe in a god 'out there', as in a super-being from outer space. So it becomes very difficult to understand what it is, exactly, that they believe to exist: the content of their (a) beliefs is obscure. They seem to want to say that there *is* something with certain characteristics, but it is not clear whether this is an 'outside power', or something in their own minds, or some kind of fictitious person or picture of a person, or what.

I do not propose (because I do not think it possible) to try to dredge up any kind of clarity from this muddle: for different believers mean different things, and many do not seem to know *what* they mean. Fortunately we need not try. For, since they do have a religion and worship *something*, there must be something that they worship – even if the hard facts about it are different from what they suppose. Perhaps what they worship is only a picture in their own minds: still, the picture exists, even if what it represents does not. I am not saying that it is not important, for such an individual, to determine just *what* he believes to exist: but it is far more important to determine whether what he believes to exist is worth *worshipping*. A man's (a) beliefs may be obscure; but this only makes his (b) beliefs more significant.

Ideals, outlooks and semi-religions

Now that we have seen that the concept of religion depends specifically on awe and worship, we can safely go on to look at the many different ideals and outlooks which people have. In Part II we shall go into more detail: here we only need to notice certain logical points about them, which should shed some light on religion as well as on the ideals and outlooks themselves.

It is true that not everybody has a *religion*, because not everybody both feels awe towards some religious object (god) and wishes to endorse and celebrate this feeling by institutionalized *worship*. But nevertheless everybody has some kind of 'outlook' on life: some picture of the world, or some set of values, or some ideal, which he more or less consciously entertains and follows. This outlook may be very well-articulated and definite: examples of this would be the Japanese code of bushido, the rules laid down for 'knightly', 'chivalrous' or 'honourable' conduct in the Middle Ages, the doctrines and precepts of Marxists or Fascists, and so on. These we might call 'metaphysical' outlooks: they have a full set of doctrines, creeds, codes and a complete world-picture. Or the outlook may be more loosely structured, and vague: those who pursue pleasure, or money, or status in society, seem to have some kind of picture or set of values according to which they live, but not a very clearly-defined one – they have no sacred book, or set of rules.

If we are interested in the *logic* and *rationality* of religion and these other outlooks (not, in this Part, in various historical and other facts about them), then it should strike us that the basic elements in these outlooks is also to be found in the emotions. Those who believe in some ideal of 'honour' feel *pride* when they live up to it, *shame* when they do not; to a Puritan, sex is connected with *fear* and *guilt*: just as to religious believers certain objects seem *awesome* or *reverend*. Modern revolutionaries find present-day society *disgusting* or *corrupting*; Arabs and others feel *hate* and *envy* for the Jews; the Nazis who believed in an ideal of 'Germany' or 'German destiny' saw Hitler and the Aryan race as *glorious* and 'inferior' races as *contemptible*.

Note that, for the most part, those who hold certain ideals do not *choose* to feel these emotions: it is usually truer to say that the emotions *overtake* them. They just *find themselves* being awed or disgusted by something, feeling ashamed or guilty or envious. This is as true of religion as of other outlooks. Not many people actually stand, balanced and uncommitted, in front of various ideals and religions, and then decide to adopt one or the other. No doubt this is what they ought to do: but it is not what happens. What happens is that the crucial emotional moves are made very early on – sometimes without the people even being conscious that they are making them: then afterwards, a whole body of beliefs, rituals, desires, doctrines and overt behaviour crystalizes round the original emotions.

'Making sense' of the world

Earlier we noticed the tendency of many people to talk in terms of 'ultimate concern', 'the meaning of life' and so forth: and we dismissed it for the time being as not essentially religious. But we can now see how it fits in. Although not everybody talks in these words, everybody has to *come to terms with* their world and their lives in some way. For the world and life do not consist just of physical objects: things in the world also affect us emotionally, and we have to have some more or less constant and adequate emotional outlook if we are to survive and be happy. When people talk of 'the meaning of life', it is this sort of thing they are really talking about.

People find various 'answers' to 'questions' about 'the meaning of life' along the lines we have noticed – that is, they adopt some religious or non-religious outlook or ideal or set of values. I put 'answers' and 'questions' in inverted commas, because they are not really answers and questions at all, in the way that 'London' and 'What is the capital of England?', or 'a table' and 'What is the meaning of "mensa" in Latin?' are answers and questions. They are rather *remedies* against the apparent 'meaninglessness' or pointlessness or boredom or anxiety of life: an attempt to 'make sense of', i.e. make worthwhile, our years of living. For instance, when Judy Garland in *The Wizard of Oz* sadly sings 'Birds fly over the rainbow: why, oh, why can't I?' this is not a serious *question*: we should not answer it by saying 'You're too heavy'. But such remarks are serious as expressions of emotion: as laments, symptoms of anxiety or worry, etc.

But people differ, of course, in the kind of 'answer' they give themselves. It is not just that they have different sorts of ideals, religions and so on, but also (as we noticed) that some people seem more anxious than others to have some *all-embracing* or complete outlook, some 'metaphysic' which covers the whole of their lives. For some, 'the Church' or 'the Party' may claim direction over all their emotions and behaviour: whereas for others ideals are essentially part-time – perhaps kept only for Sundays. Some people are more totally 'committed' or 'dedicated' than others: it is not only the nature but the extent or power of the outlook that is different.

A parallel
It is very easy to be vague and cloudy about the way emotions enter into large-scale ideals, outlooks, and religions; so perhaps it will be useful to look at a more familiar example of what I have called 'emotional investment' in some object. It is like, though not of course the same as, investing an object (god) with the emotion

of awe, worshipping it and having a religion; and its familiarity may enable us to see more clearly how we should tackle various problems.

This is the example of someone who is romantically in love with someone else: say, a boy with his girl-friend. Now when the boy is head-over-heels in love, he will speak about her in quite a different way. To him she is a goddess, the incarnation of all beauty and goodness, infinitely desirable, superhuman. As with religion, he has (a) certain emotions about her, (b) certain beliefs, and (c) certain characteristic ways of behaving, all of which are different from the people who are not in love with her. He (a) feels passionately, loving, needing, humble, perhaps in awe; (b) believes she is marvellous, beautiful, etc.; (c) has certain rituals which express his love, such as kissing the pillow, cherishing her love-letters, buying her presents, and so on.

Just as we asked what was specifically *religious* about cases of actual religions, so we can ask what is specific to 'being in love' in these cases. Here too it is not a matter of different moral, or scientific, or historical beliefs – the man in love may have just the same beliefs of this kind about her as anyone else has. The difference lies in the emotion, or the emotion-based attitude, from which flows everything that the boy does in relation to her. If the boy wrote poetry to or about her, it would be absurd to take the poetry as stating historical or moral or scientific facts: what the poetry does is to express his attitude.

Now before moving on to the next chapter, in which we shall take a look at the reason and unreason of religion, note that (1) being in love is often not a matter of choice – rather, it *overtakes* people: (2) it is often useless to *argue* with someone in love, because his emotions are too compulsive and overwhelming to allow him to look at it reasonably: (3) like the religious believer, he 'believes in' or 'has faith in' the girl he loves – and this again is a matter of attitude or commitment. Nevertheless, (4) – and this is very important – we do think that 'being in love' is connected with being reasonable or unreasonable, sane or insane. You can fall in love with 'the wrong girl' (perhaps one who will make you very unhappy): or one might think that 'being (romantically) in love' was itself rather like being temporarily insane: or you might come to see, not so much by argument but by seeing things (or the girl) in a different light, that your romantic passion was misplaced or misguided – that your emotional attitude to the girl was *mistaken*.

It is fairly easy to see, in this case, how 'what is reasonable' does come into the matter: how it is not enough to say 'Oh, well, it's a matter of taste'. The same is true of religion: *religion too is within the scope of reason*. We shall try to see what this means in the next chapter.

three

Religion and Reason

MANY PEOPLE react to arguments about religion by saying such things as 'Religion is a matter of faith, not reason': 'It's not a rational matter, there's no point in arguing about it': 'It's just a matter of taste, everyone picks the religion that suits him', and so on. It is very important to see why such remarks are misguided.

First, the remarks *may* be saying something true and sensible. As we saw in the parallel with 'being in love' at the end of the last chapter, it is true

(1) that usually people *are* not reasonable about their religion – either in adopting it, or in defending it against critics
(2) that different religions may be 'right' for different people
(3) that the *kind* of reason and unreason which applies to religion is not like the kind of reason and unreason which applies to other things: it may not, for instance, lend itself to deductive argument in the way that geometry does, or to the sort of evidence and arguments we use in science or history.

But some of this entitles us to say that religion is not within the scope of reason. Thus (1) although people *are* not often reasonable about it, this does not show that they *ought* not to be reasonable: (2) although different religions may suit different people (as different medicines do), it may still be true that *some* religions may be wrong for everybody, and also that for each individual person there is a right and wrong choice to be made (just as poisons kill everybody, and each patient needs the right medicine – not just any medicine – for him).

I suspect that these simple truths are overlooked only because people feel lost, depressed and despairing about the possibility of bringing reason to bear on religion. The whole thing seems too difficult, and the only methods which immediately occur to one seem obviously useless – rather as one could have a school subject called 'Who you ought to fall in love with', but would it do any good or make any real difference to anybody? So we can ask questions like 'Should you be a Roman Catholic (Protestant, Communist, etc.)?', but wouldn't the resulting talk just be a waste of time, because people have really made up their minds in advance? Hence we feel tempted to give the whole thing up, and say 'You can't do anything – it's not a rational matter'.

Yet at the same time, in our saner moments, we know very well that some religions and outlooks and ideals *are* unreasonable – sometimes even insane. We do not think that 'it's just a matter of taste' if a Nazi worships Hitler and spends his time killing and torturing Jews, or if a Baal-worshipper insists on sacrificing infants on the altar of his god. We think these people are wrong, misguided, mistaken, unreasonable, prejudiced, fanatical and so forth. All these words imply some kind of *standards* or criteria which are objective, in that they apply to all human beings and do not just express how we feel about it.

This is the crucial point at which, both in the particular case of religion and in all other departments of human life, people have the choice of jumping one way or the other. One thing you can do is to reject reason altogether and all the words that go along with it – 'evidence', 'grounds', 'sensible', 'prejudiced', 'sane', 'mistake', etc. and a host of others. You can just *not think*, not go in for the normal human activity of making up one's mind on the evidence, considering the facts, being logical and so on. You can contradict yourself, not listen to what other people say, not face your own feelings, and not observe the usual rules of discussion and argument. You can do this not only about religion, but about any other part of life – your personal problems, the problems of society, your relationships with parents, friends, teachers and others, even with your work and career. This involves withdrawing not only from thinking, but also from talking or communicating. If you did this all the time, you would be more like an autistic child or a lunatic than a human being.

Most people do this some of the time (particularly when things get difficult, and they are too depressed, or too lazy, or too anxious to think). But most (sane) people jump the other way, at least in principle; that is, they believe that they *ought* to be reasonable and to think, even if they sometimes find it difficult. They believe that they ought to use evidence, to be sensible, guided by the facts of the world outside rather than by their inner desires and fantasies, and so on; in a word, that they ought to be reasonable. If a person does not believe this as a matter of principle, there is no point talking or arguing with him (and certainly no point in writing a book for him to read): for the whole business of talk, argument and debate depend on the notion that there are such things as reasons to which we ought to attend.

In the case of religious believers, it is sometimes very difficult to know which of these two ways they would jump. One author, for example, says 'If a man chooses Roman Catholicism or some other form of Christianity or some atheistic view of the world, he does so because, confronted with that view as a whole, he feels in himself that this view is the best . . . There is no religious (or anti-religious) view of the Universe which can be demonstrated with logical necessity from generally admitted premises. Whatever hypothesis regarding the Ground of the Universe a man adopts, he makes a leap beyond experience'.[1] In this passage it sometimes seems that the author believes that one view can be *better* than another, or a correct 'hypothesis': which of course implies that there are *reasons why* it is better or correct. But at other times it seems that he does not believe this: you have to 'make a leap', the view cannot be 'demonstrated', etc.

Naturally one would like to force such people to make their minds up. For, in the last resort, they must jump one way or the other; either they are going to arrive at their views by considering reasons, evidence, and so on, or else they are not – in which case they will choose the one they feel drawn towards, or pick one at random. But such people will not be forced. For they want *both* to hang on to their particular religious beliefs, *and* at the same time to seem reasonable. But, as we have seen, one of these two must have priority. A man's ultimate allegiance must be given either to

[1] Edwyn Bevan in *Christianity* (Thornton Butterworth, Home University Library, pp. 247–50).

the notions of reason, evidence, etc., or to a particular set of beliefs. We cannot have it both ways.

What kind of reason?

Most sane people want to be reasonable. But it is understandable that they are not clear about what counts as being reasonable in the area of religion – what sort of reasons are relevant. Thus, in the passage just quoted, the author claims that no religious view of the Universe 'can be demonstrated with logical necessity'. But perhaps 'logical necessity' is not the *sort* of way in which we should try to 'demonstrate' the rightness of religious beliefs.

Indeed this is plainly the case. Some of us have a picture of 'reason' which includes only *certain forms* of reason. Most commonly, as in the above example, the picture includes only strict logical deduction: the sort of thing we get in geometry and mathematics generally. Here we can prove things in a very strong sense of 'prove': that is, we can show them to be true with absolute, 100% certainty. Given the axioms of Euclid, or the meaning of mathematical signs like 2, and 2, and 4, and =, there is absolutely no doubt that the three angles of a triangle add up to 180 degrees, or that 2 plus 2 equals 4.

But of course this is only one kind of 'proof' or 'reasoning'. Scientists use another kind. It *might* be the case that the world is flat, or that the earth does not go round the sun: that is, it would not be *nonsense* to say such things, as it would be nonsense (given the rules of mathematics) to say that 2 and 2 made 5. But we can still *prove*, with the sort of proof that scientists use and we accept, that the world is round and goes round the sun. We are *certain* of it: there is good *evidence* for it, and so on.

There are a great many kinds of proof – as many as there are areas of human thought and inquiry. Proof of a man's guilt in a law-court is different again from both mathematics and science: proof of the wrongness of killing people, or of the imprudence of smoking too many cigarettes, or of the merits of some books and music and paintings as against others, are all different. But – this is the temptation we must avoid – this does not mean that some are better or worse than others: we must not think that only certain kinds of proof (perhaps the mathematical kind) is 'really' proof, and that the rest are just inferior forms of it. None is better or worse than the others: they are just different. Why ever should we expect to prove things in the area of morals, or religion, or works of art *by the same methods* as we prove things in mathematics or science?

Note also one other point: that the methods of proof in some of these forms of human thought do not always involve what we might strictly call *argument*. If I am out to prove to you that Molly is a better girl to marry than Flossie, or that you would enjoy going to Spain for a holiday more than to Blackpool, what am I likely to do? Well, certainly I may talk and argue to some extent: but I may also do things like showing you films and pictures of Spain, tell you stories about Molly and Flossie, perhaps get you to read novels in which people like Molly and Flossie appear, arrange a meeting with them in particular circumstances, bring in a Spaniard for you to talk to, and so forth.

It does not matter much whether we want to call such moves 'arguments' or 'proof'. The point is that I do these things in order to give you more evidence, to show you in a reasonable way what the position is. I do not browbeat you, or indoctrinate you, or put any kind of non-rational pressure on you: I just try to show you what Molly and Flossie, Spain and Blackpool, are like. Perhaps you have some false picture of them which the films and stories will correct, or perhaps you simply do not know enough about them to make up your mind intelligently. All this is part of the process of bringing your choice more within the scope of reason, more guided by the evidence.

Reason and the emotions
Once we see this, we shall be at least more willing to admit that the notion of 'being reasonable' may have more application to religion than we thought at first. We saw in the last chapter that religion was, basically and centrally, a matter of a certain kind of 'emotional investment': that the religious believer saw certain things in the world (gods) as deserving of an emotion-based attitude – an attitude of awe and worship. To this the believer will add other emotions: he will think that he ought to feel guilty about certain things, revere and count sacred certain things, and

so forth. At this point we shall, I hope, be less tempted to say 'If it's a matter of emotion, what's it got to do with reason?'

This *is* a temptation; but we can now see that emotions can be reasonable or unreasonable, and that there may be proofs or reasons which show them to be so. When we say things like 'He's unreasonably angry' or 'She's unreasonably unhappy' or 'She's unreasonably jealous' or 'They have good reason to be afraid', we are not talking nonsense. We may not be able to prove the truth of what we say by 'pure logic', as we do in mathematics: but we may be able to prove it by other methods. Our task now is to see what these other methods are.

We cannot do this just by concentrating on the specifically religious emotions of awe and reverence and all that goes to make up worship. What we need is some general picture of the ways in which we can be reasonable or unreasonable in the sphere of the emotions: a picture of the kinds of mistakes we can make in this area. In doing this we shall not be straying too far from religion; for as we have said, almost all the emotions (not just awe) *come into* various religions – and not only into religions, but also into 'metaphysical' outlooks generally: Communism, an ideal of 'honour', the outlooks of conformists and rebels in our society, and so on.

Conscious and unconscious beliefs

Perhaps the most obvious way in which a person can be unreasonable in his emotions is if his feeling is based on a false belief. For instance, if I think my wife has slept with another man, I may be jealous; but if in fact she has not, then my jealousy is unreasonable because my belief is false. Nazis who believed that Hitler would bring Germany to victory, and that the Jews were plotting to overthrow the state, worshipped and admired Hitler and hated the Jews; but, since Hitler was a disaster for Germany and Jews were not plotting, these beliefs were false, and hence the worship, admiration and hate were unreasonable.

There are many cases of this kind. But unfortunately there are just as many cases of a different and more complicated kind. Perhaps this can best be illustrated by the example of race prejudice that we have just used. There are indeed some people who have false *conscious* beliefs about the Jews, Negroes, etc. They are prepared to come right out and say things like 'They are plotting to overthrow us', 'They don't feel pain like we do', 'They are nearer the animals', 'Don't trust them with your daughters', and so on. But more commonly racially-prejudiced people will not admit, *even to themselves*, that they have such beliefs. Consciously, they will agree that Jews are not plotting, Negroes feel pain and other sensations just like we do, are just as trustworthy, and so on. But their whole way of talking and behaving shows us quite clearly that they don't *really* believe this. The passion that comes into their voices when they speak of Jews and Negroes, their facial symptoms and bodily postures, and above all their actual behaviour towards them, all convince us that they are prejudiced – even if they sometimes produce what seem to be good reasons for their behaviour.

These people have false *unconscious* beliefs. They will not admit the beliefs, perhaps because they are ashamed of having them. To use another example in my own experience: when I was about 13 I was supposed to learn how to swim at school. I was frightened of the bigger boys and the water, thinking that I might get drowned or bullied. Of course I did not like admitting this fear, because it would seem cowardly; and almost at once I stopped admitting it *to myself*. I went around saying, both to myself and to other people, things like 'Oh, no, I'm not *frightened* of swimming, it's just so *boring*. I'd much rather do something else'. And whenever I was supposed to have a swimming lesson, I arranged to have a cough or a cold or something else that would let me out of it.

Here I was *unconsciously afraid* of learning to swim, unconsciously believing that it would be dangerous. It was not until a teacher who knew me well, and whom I trusted, said something like 'Come on John, you're not really bored by it, really you're a bit scared, aren't you?' that I was able to admit, to him and to myself, that I *was* frightened. Even then I did not like to admit it: it took a long time to build up the relationship of trust with the teacher which would enable me to be (in a deep sense) honest with myself, and hence with other people. After that, learning to swim was easy, because I was able to say 'Look, I'm very nervous about this, so don't grab hold of me in the water', and so on.

One more example, nearer to the specifically religious emotions: many teenagers, as they afterwards admit when they are grown up, feel uncertain and insecure. They wonder whether they are strong, potent, able to cope with the world, able to meet adults on equal terms. This is a humiliating feeling: nobody likes to see himself as weak, anxious, worried, in need of protection. So they deny, even to themselves, that this is what they feel. Instead they pretend (still to themselves as well as to others) that they are big, tough, strong, potent, daring and so on. They rush around on powerful motorbikes, or behave violently towards other people: really in an endeavour to prove to themselves that they *are* strong. They may admire, even worship, a hero-figure who is a really 'tough guy': someone who represents what they would be like if they could.

In this example, the worship of the hero is virtually a kind of religion. Here we can see how it arises, and how complex the position is. It arises from the *unconscious* or *repressed* feelings of inferiority, weakness, etc. that the teenagers have, and the subsequent necessity for them to *pretend* otherwise. This may end up with a kind of 'tough guy' religion, or an 'honour' ethic, in which 'not losing face', 'not backing down' (as with gunfighters in Western films), 'being brave', and so on are the chief elements in a code, rather like the code of the Japanese samurai. The point here is that (a) the unreason of this stems from the failure to own up to the original unconscious beliefs, and (b) any method of convincing the teenager that he was unreasonable would not proceed by overt argument, but rather by getting him to face these beliefs.

In the same sort of way, we may make plausible guesses about particular religions. Suppose that somebody relies enormously on his father: he regards his father as powerful, all-wise, as protecting him against the world and solving his problems for him. This would happen when he was a young child; and perhaps fairly soon this belief in an omnipotent and omniscient father becomes unconscious — he has this picture deep in his mind, but is not aware of it. Then his father dies or lets him down in some way (perhaps by making a mistake): but the unconscious need is still there, so the person invents and worships a god who will satisfy the need, a god who fits the picture. This would be an all-powerful father-god, like the sort of god we get in many religions.

Of course this is over-simple; the various emotions and beliefs that make up particular religions are far more complex than that. But these examples will at least show that the kinds of unreason in religion and in our emotional lives generally are very deep-rooted and hard to get at: that being reasonable about religion and the emotions is not just a matter of strictly logical argument at the conscious level, but is likely to be much more a matter of facing our own (hidden) feelings. This, incidentally, is why so many arguments about religion never seem to get off the ground: they deal with the 'surface' beliefs and feelings, but do not touch the hidden beliefs and feelings which are the real basis of a man's religion. Yet at the same time we should now see that these hidden beliefs, like any other beliefs, are amenable to reason – if we can get at them.

four

Should One have a Religion?

WE HAVE now a somewhat clearer picture about what sort of thing religion is, and how the notion of being reasonable/unreasonable may apply to particular religious beliefs, and other beliefs which go along with emotionally-based 'pictures of the world'. In other words, we are beginning to have some idea about what it means to be reasonable or unreasonable *within* a religion, or in choosing between one religion and another. We can see, if only dimly, how worshipping Hitler might be unreasonable, because involving the belief that awe and admiration are appropriate for Hitler: and now worshipping some truly great and good man might be, at least, *more* reasonable – since such a man would be a worthier target for such emotions.

But before going into more detail, we need to look at the more general question of whether one ought to have a religion *at all*. Perhaps it is more reasonable, or less obviously insane, to worship (say) Jesus rather than Hitler: but is it reasonable to be in awe and worship in general? Are these not feelings and activities which we ought to grow out of, as unworthy of adult human beings? No doubt we ought to *respect*, *admire* or *value* certain people, or certain institutions, or other objects of our emotions (great works of art, for instance): but ought we to *worship* them?

We must first clear away a number of points that may prevent us from getting down to this question:

(a) First, we have to grant that 'having a religion' is not an inevitable thing for all human beings. Admittedly, all human beings have some sort of more or less well-articulated 'world picture', or 'set of values': that is, they have some kind of emotional investment in various parts of the world, in virtue of which they behave in certain ways – they may follow Hitler, or honour, or pleasure, or the Communist Party, or their own inner feelings, or almost anything. But they do not all *worship* something. That represents a further step which a man may or may not take. I can feel admiration, respect, love, and almost anything else towards Jesus: but if Jesus is to figure in my *religion* I must *worship* him. So the question 'Should one have a religion?' is a real question, amounting to 'Are being in awe and worshipping desirable activities for human beings?'

(b) But secondly, remembering what we said in Chapter 1 about what religion is *not*, we can see that the question 'Should one have a religion?' is not to be answered in the light of the history or common practice of particular religions. To have a religion is not (1) to pick Christianity or one of the 'higher' religions, (2) to adopt a particular moral code, (3) to go in for magical or pseudo-scientific beliefs, (4) to have 'religious experiences', (5) to engage in common rituals, (6) to have some 'ultimate concern', or (7) to accept certain historical facts. We can be in awe of, and worship, something without doing *any* of these. Thus, to be dissuaded from religion in general on the grounds that particular religions have often advocated bad morals (2), or have clashed with science (3), is just mistaken. This may mean that a particular religion has been contaminated, but not that religion as a whole is undesirable.

(c) Thirdly, we are not here concerned with whether religion is desirable for some external or *extrinsic* reason. Thus some people say that, without religion, our morality or our civilization will decline: or that people will be unhappier: or that religion is the only thing that keeps some men sane: or that, in the present state of society, religious organizations serve a useful or essential function. These, and many other, reasons have been advanced for the desirability of religion. But we do not want to know whether religion is *useful* for certain external purposes – purposes which might, after all, be served just as well or better by other devices. We want to know whether it is *reasonable*: whether it is the sort of thing a sane man, and a sane society, would go in for.

The question is, then, whether awe and worship are desirable. It is a very hard question, and it will be best to begin by looking more closely at the notion of awe. Awe is characteristically felt about things or people who are *overwhelmingly impressive,* before which we feel *small*, or *humble*. If one is in awe, one does not necessarily *fear* the thing, or *obey* it, or feel *dependent* on it: but one regards it as mighty, majestic, a source of power and mystery, not something to be exploited but something before which one should feel *passive*, taking in and being moved by its majesty and impressiveness. We may have such a feeling towards our parents when we are young, towards great works of art, the starry heavens above, the wonder of the universe, or almost anything. In such cases, we feel that merely to *respect* or *admire* or *appreciate* the object is an insufficient response: it would be as if, when confronted with the glories of outer space, or a majestic cathedral, or a wonderful piece of music, we merely said 'Ah, yes, how charming!'

Those who consider the notion of awe undesirable have usually been misled by supposing that human beings can only adopt *one* attitude to any object: as if we could *either* be in awe of the stars and outer space, *or* investigate them and exploit them scientifically, but not both. Then, thinking (rightly) that scientific investigation is a good thing, such people suppose that an attitude of awe, reverence, etc. must be a bad thing because it must impede science. But this is a mistake. Obviously I can at one time be in awe of the stars, but at another time investigate them by astronomy: just as at one time I can be overwhelmed by the majesty of a cathedral, and at another time go into the question of how, as a piece of engineering, it manages to stand up straight.

One straightforward argument for the desirability of awe is that those who do not feel it seem to be missing something. There is, surely, something about some things in the world – though of course one might argue about *which* things – that *is* overwhelming. You may find it in great music, I in nature, Smith in Jesus Christ, Jones in Hitler, and so on. If a person reacted to *nothing* in this way, we should probably think that he was in some respect deficient. Those who have any experience, and are *open* to having experience, of these objects, do in fact react with awe. The man who travels only in a safe ocean liner may miss the majesty of the sea; but the man who really *meets* the sea and is not simply concerned with *using* it is likely to feel at least respect, and probably awe – he may even turn it into a god and call it Neptune.

Often we feel that the people who are deficient in this way are not just lacking something, but have positively *repressed* something. It may not be so much lack of understanding, but fear of his own feelings, that makes a man say things like 'Awe? Good heavens, no, *I'm* not in awe of anything'. And in fact he may seem to himself to be without the emotion. Yet we can see, in his behaviour and his tone of voice and other things, that there are some things of which he is, unconsciously, in awe. It may be his boss, or his wife, or people of a superior social class or status, or anything. He does not like the idea of being in awe, perhaps because it makes him feel child-like, vulnerable, insecure: he prefers a picture of himself as totally independent, not impressed too much by anything or anybody. But it is a false picture.

This raises the interesting possibility that awe may be something *inevitable* for human beings. Of course not everybody admits to awe, or carries it over into worship and religion; but it may be that everybody is bound to feel it. As a small child, at least, each person is plainly going to find a great deal about the world overwhelming, large, powerful, majestic: most obviously, the objects of awe will include the child's parents – which is why many religions clearly reflect the ways in which religious believers saw their parents – but they may include other things as well. It seems possible to maintain that, provided we are completely honest, awe is something we could not (in principle) ever grow out of entirely. For there will always be some things, even if they are buried deeply in our unconscious minds as images, which we continue to find overwhelmingly impressive.

Of course these things may change; and the kind of change may be represented in this history of some religions. Thus we may come to think that some of our more primitive, naïve gods, who hurl thunderbolts and so on, are not awesome: or even that we have no need to be in awe of some 'father-god in the sky'. But we shall still feel, perhaps, that such things as love, the power of human emotions and the majesty of the human reason, are worthy of more than just respect or admiration – that they are mighty, potent, impressive, awesome. We may realize that our attitude to such things cannot, if we are honest, *only* be that of the scientist. For with regard to these things, at least, we are not and can never be in full control, or in a position of superiority. So although the objects of awe may change, it is at least arguable that awe is something 'given': as, indeed, all the basic emotions are 'given' and inevitable. *What* we love, fear, hate, etc. may alter, and should alter, as we acquire more understanding: but *that* we should love, fear and hate is part of being human.

If this is so, what follows for religion? What seems to follow is that we should accept the inevitability and desirability of awe, recognizing its importance for human life: and, if we do this, that we should wish to express and 'institutionalize' it, by means of worship. For if I think that some object, X, is a worthy recipient of awe – if I think that it is right and important that I and others should have this attitude to X – then I will naturally find some way of *showing* this. In order to keep the feeling alive, and remind myself of its importance, I will devise occasions of expressing and endorsing the awe – that is, occasions of worship. And if other people feel the same as I do, we shall 'institutionalize' the worship: that is, we shall have institutions and set forms (perhaps a church service) which fulfil this function. All this will plainly be sensible.

Of course this is precisely what various religions have done in practice. And there is a sort of parallel with other things that we cannot quite call religions. For instance, if I think that my country is important, and that it is right to have certain feelings about it, then I will have set forms and ceremonies (saluting the flag, etc.) in which this patriotism can find expression. If I believe in the importance of some moral or social cause, I have meetings and protest marches. Even if I only love money, I may spend a lot of time in rituals which demonstrate this – as misers count their gold, for instance. Provided we are right about the worthiness of the object, as a recipient for these feelings, the 'institutionalization' is obviously desirable.

But this is just where, in practice, particular religions seem to fail us. We have a large number of religions and quasi-religions, worshipping particular gods or other religious objects, from which we can choose. Yet few of them are very much concerned with showing that it is *reasonable* to worship their particular objects. They are concerned with maintaining the faith of their existing adherents, or with acquiring new adherents by processes of indoctrination, oratory, missionizing, propaganda, and so forth: but not with *explaining why*, in their view, any reasonable and sensible person should worship what they worship.

This points to what is perhaps the basic defect in religions as we have them, a defect which makes further progress in religion very difficult. It is that, consciously or unconsciously, most religious believers feel that the kind of questions with which we are here concerned *should not be asked*. It seems that we are not supposed to stand before various religions, balanced and uncommitted, and inquire whether it is sensible to worship this or that god: we are supposed rather to 'make a leap of faith', 'have a commitment', or *be overtaken by* religious belief. Yet plainly to act in this way is a mark of insanity rather than sanity.

The feeling is, I think, that it is somehow presumptuous or out of place to conduct any serious inquiry into what we ought to worship, or what forms our worship should take. Of course religious believers themselves do, up to a point, conduct such inquiries: but nearly always against an existing background of belief, commitment, and obedience to some traditional authority. The idea of *starting from scratch*, or of *deciding* what forms of worship to use (rather than making slight changes on a traditional pattern), seems almost blasphemous.

Yet some such serious inquiry is what is needed. If awe is inevitable or desirable, we need to decide what our objects of awe *ought* to be – what objects are appropriate. The critical inquiry must precede any commitment. Having done this – difficult enough, surely, to last us for some time! – we need to determine what institutional forms of worship best suit human psychology. There have been one or two scattered attempts to do this in human history, usually when a particular religious tradition breaks down (as after the French Revolution, when there was a movement to worship Reason and erect Temples of Reason); and some modern psychologists have been interested in the subject. But such attempts have not been, for the most part, either serious or successful: and one reason why they have not is that it requires *both* a sympathetic concern for religion in general, *and* a willingness to stand back from all particular religions. This is an attitude which few people can manage.

The decline of organized Christianity in many industrialized societies, such as the U.K. and the U.S.A., has naturally led to many quasi-religious groups of people who are 'seeking their own salvation', as a religious believer would put it, by various methods. Some attach themselves to drugs, others to violent protest, others to various forms of meditation or highly generalized ideals like 'peace', 'love', etc. Unfortunately their (justifiable) dissatisfaction with existing religions has not led them to take the job of reconstruction seriously. The questions we have asked – what should we be in awe of, what should we worship and in what forms should we worship it? – require a great deal of hard philosophical thinking, and a great deal of psychological knowledge, if we are to have any hope of answering them correctly. It is only in this kind of seriousness that we can place any confidence for future progress.

five

Right and Wrong in Religion

IN THIS final chapter of Part I, we need to inspect in more detail the various ways in which a person can be reasonable or unreasonable, go right or go wrong, in religious beliefs. In Chapter 3, we saw how this might (in a general way) be possible, and we there saw also the crucial importance of the emotions to religious belief: in Chapter 4, we showed how having *some* religion – that is, worshipping something – might be a reasonable thing (again in general) to do. So it becomes a matter of urgency to get clearer about the *criteria* or standards by which we should judge religious beliefs and emotions as good or bad, sane or insane, reasonable or unreasonable.

But first a word of warning (or comfort). The process of making a reasonable decision about what to worship, or how to direct one's religious emotions, is one which each person must undertake for himself. It is the same here with religion as it is with morals, or indeed with any other rational undertaking. Not much would be gained by having a team of experts who, after a good deal of research, ended by saying: 'Right, well, we have done all the work and *this* (PQR) is the sort of thing you ought to worship, and *these* (XYZ) are the ways in which you ought to worship: so now go and get on with it'. Of course we would respect and value their opinion: but we would need to see for ourselves *why* that opinion was right (if indeed it was).

In just the same way an expert mathematician can tell us the answers to problems (or we can look them up in the back of the book): or an expert art critic can tell us which pictures we should admire: but in neither case would we have learned anything about mathematics or art, just by listening to the experts. We would have to work out for ourselves why the answer was such-

and-such, or to appreciate the points about the pictures which are admirable. So too in morality and religion. Giving people 'the right answers' is not much use in itself. What they need is not answers, but help and encouragement in getting their own answers: or more precisely, a set of principles and methods whereby they can get their own answers – the techniques required to find things out for themselves.

This connects with what I said in the first paragraph. Rather than issuing statements like 'We all ought to worship so-and-so', I shall try to make clear the criteria or standards by which we would most sensibly judge what to worship, or more generally whether our emotions are rightly disposed. These criteria or standards are not the monopoly of any religion, or any anti-religious group: they are just part of what it means to be reasonable in this area. So I am not selling my own beliefs or values, or any other person's. What we need here is to get clear about the various ways in which mistakes are possible.

These various ways need to be tabulated; I shall do this by using one example throughout, the example of a person who worships (admires, reveres, etc.) Hitler. I, choose this because it is (I hope) an agreed case of somebody worshipping the wrong sort of person: but if anybody disagrees, it does not matter – for the *kind* of mistakes should still be obvious. Let us suppose, then, that we are dealing with a person who thinks that Hitler is a god, or acts as if he thinks so. How many different things are there that might have gone wrong?

(1) He might simply *not know the facts* about Hitler. Thus, to anyone who has read (say) Alan Bullock's book about Hitler, it would be difficult to admire someone who, as this historian clearly shows, was responsible for many murders. But our person, perhaps, does not know this: Hitler has concealed it from him, and he has been misinformed, told that Hitler was not responsible.

(2) He might be incompetent at knowing *what Hitler feels*. Suppose he is right about all the 'hard facts' about Hitler – he knows exactly what Hitler actually did, what he was responsible for – yet he may still be wrong about Hitler's feelings, motives and intentions. He might, for instance, accept that it was with sorrow and

pity that Hitler 'felt obliged' to kill millions of Jews, or to invade Russia, or enslave half Europe. He might fail to realize that Hitler is the sort of person who likes doing this sort of thing.

(3) He might be incompetent at knowing *what his own feelings are*. For instance, if he is a very anxious and insecure person, he may in fact attach himself to Hitler because Hitler seems to him to be big, strong, a powerful orator, and so forth. He sees in Hitler a 'big brother', or an all-powerful father, who will lift him out of his insecurity. But if he had realized to the full his own feelings of insecurity, he would have been less eager to see Hitler in that light: and perhaps more able to tolerate those feelings on his own, without the need to search for another person to carry them for him.

(4) More subtly, he might not make any of the above mistakes, yet still go wrong by allowing himself to be carried away *at the time*. Let us try to put this more precisely. The man could (1) know the facts about Hitler, (2) know Hitler's feelings, and (3) know his own feelings, and yet not *bring this knowledge to bear* in his everyday life. He might be carried away by the emotion of the Nazi rallies, or so eager to satisfy his own feelings that he never stops to look at them, or just too lazy to use the valuable knowledge that he has. This is the case where the man *can* think straight, if he only stopped to think: but in fact he never stops to think at all.

(5) More subtly still, he may have all the knowledge in (1), (2) and (3), and bring it to bear as in (4), yet still find himself in awe of Hitler and worshipping him. Despite all that he can consciously do, the emotion still persists in him. He might say 'Yes, I know Hitler isn't the right sort of person to feel admiration and awe for, but somehow I just do – I can't help it'. This would mean that he has some *unconscious* belief that Hitler is an appropriate object of worship: he knows consciously that this is silly, but unconsciously he is driven into it against his will, much as one might continue to be in love with somebody who one knows, consciously, to be the wrong sort of person.

These five ways of going wrong, or five types of unreason, are all very important. To make sure I have put them clearly, let us take another case where emotions are involved – not a case of religion. Suppose I am the sort of person who hates coloured people (say, Pakistanis) and goes around beating them up. Then:

(1) I may just be ignorant of the facts. I may think that they are plotting to overthrow the state, or assassinate all white people (perhaps some wicked uncle has told me this): so that I think it right to beat them up, in the public interest. (Some people seem to have thought this sort of thing about the Jews in Nazi Germany.)
(2) I may believe that coloured people don't feel pain as white people do, or that they rather enjoy being beaten up. (This sounds lunatic, but again many people have talked as if they believed it.)
(3) More plausibly, I may not be clear about my own feelings. I may be the sort of person who so hates the kind of life I am living that I feel I must protest and kick against it, and the only way I can do this is to hit someone else: or I may unconsciously feel small and inferior, and need to prove my strength and status by conquering and beating other people.
(4) Again plausibly, I may be clear about the truth of (1), (2) and (3) above, yet fail to bring that truth before my mind at the time. When I am with my mates in a back-street with a Pakistani, I just don't stop to think: I get carried away, and beat him up.
(5) I may not fall victim to any of (1)–(4) above, and yet still find myself hating coloured people. In this case I shall probably be able to restrain myself from beating them up, since I am aware – even at the time – that my hate is unreasonable. But I still may not be able to help hating them. Here there must be some unconscious belief which causes my hate.

These five types of mistakes are possible, as this example shows, not just in cases of religion, but in any case where the emotions are involved. A father gets very angry at his daughter's boy-friend because he has long hair. Is it that he really thinks long hair to be a sign of bad character? Or can't he judge the boy's character competently? Or is he ignorant of his own jealousy, of the fact that he doesn't like his daughter going out with boy-friends at all? Or does he know all this, but just 'forgets' it at the time? Or does he know it and remember it, but somehow still can't help being angry?

D

And so with all other cases – being in love, feeling guilty, and so forth. We need not produce more examples here.

In the case of religion, I incline to believe (though we cannot be certain without a good deal more research) that most of the mistakes come into (3), (4) or (5). That is, the cases where people are just wrong about the facts, or about other people's feelings, are comparatively rare. What happens is surely more often like this: a person has some kind of compulsion, or motive, or psychological need of his own. He has to attach this to something, and attaches it to something in the outside world irrespective of whether the attachment is suitable. He feels the need of a strong leader like Hitler, or of proving his strength by beating up people who look different from ourselves. He goes wrong either (3) by not knowing about his inner compulsions, or (4) by not bringing this knowledge to bear, or (5) by not being able to change this feelings in the light of that knowledge, so deeply rooted are the feelings within him.

Of (3), (4) and (5), we cannot make any guesses about which is the most frequent mistake, because they are in an important way *cumulative*. If someone (3) does not know what he feels, then of course he cannot (4) bring this knowledge to bear, or (5) be influenced by it. A person needs to go right in (3), (4) *and* (5) if he is to have the right feeling at the end: he can break down at any point. But I should say, if I had to, that most of us break down right at the beginning, in (3): that we are very unclear about what our real feelings are on such occasions. This is why, in my view, any serious attempt to improve our reasonableness as regards religion will have to start with a serious attempt to improve our self-knowledge.

How is this to be done? It is possible, and very useful, to learn more about psychology and the emotions generally from books, and then to transfer this knowledge to various existing or past religions. We can, with such knowledge, see certain things to be true about (say) the worship of Jehovah, or Hitler, or other gods: we can see, albeit dimly, what sort of emotions lie behind such worship, and how far these emotions were sensible. We can see, from the false – often, *obviously* false – beliefs which various religious believers had, how those emotions led them astray. We can ask questions like 'Why is it that some Japanese felt it better (more honourable) to commit suicide rather than be taken prisoner?', 'Why is there so much stress on purity in the book of Leviticus?', and so forth. All this is a good start, and will at least give us a clearer idea of what lies at the root of religions, behind the masks of doctrine and ritual.

But it is more important and also more difficult, to get a firm grasp of our own emotions *as individuals*. It is all very well to look down, in perhaps a superior and detached way, at the types of unreason committed by various religious believers in the past, as we may at those committed by people who are racially prejudiced, or the Nazis, or the naïve worshippers of Mao Tse-Tung. But if this gives us a cosy feeling of rational superiority, it will be worse than useless. For it is precisely the same *kind* of mistakes to which we ourselves are liable: perhaps, in this sophisticated age, in less gross and obvious forms, but still the same mistakes. We have not grown out of the unconscious compulsions, fears, anxieties and lusts that are present in the whole human race: we have, at best, altered the objects to which we attach them.

Learning more about ourselves in this way, which is an essential in the general task of deciding what sort of religion (if any) to have, is not so much a matter of deep *intellectual* study as a matter of honesty and courage. We have to *own up* to what we feel deep down within ourselves. The only really adequate way of learning here is in the company of other people whom we trust, and with whom we are able to communicate honestly and freely, so that after talking to them we know at least a little more about what we really feel. *Argument*, in the superficial sense, about religion is generally useless: but a determined and honest attempt to say what the *feelings* are on which one bases (say) one's belief in Roman Catholicism, or Marxism, or a hatred of anything religious, is immensely valuable. For only by recognizing the feelings can one begin to have any control over them.

We began, and have continued, by asking questions about religion. In Chapter 1, we cleared away some of the undergrowth by looking at the various things that religion was *not*: in Chapter 2 we were able to see that religion was essentially a matter of awe and worship, of the attachment of certain emotions to certain objects. In Chapter 3 we saw that this attachment could be reasonable and unreasonable, so that religion was within the scope of reason – even though the reasons required were not like those applied in mathematics, or science, or any other form of thinking. In Chapter 4 we considered the possibility that awe might be an inevitable human emotion, and hence that the institutionalization of it in worship – 'having a religion' – was desirable: and in Chapter 5 we considered in more detail the kind of ways in which we could go wrong in the sorts of things we worshipped or attached our emotions to.

But it should now be clear that, from the strictly logical point of view – that is, from the viewpoint of someone who wants to determine the *rationality* of particular religions – we have entered a wider field. Religion is only *one area* of life in which people make emotional attachments. In order to investigate that area, and the kinds of reason and unreason that applied to it, we had in effect to consider *in general* how we could go wrong in our emotions. It is clear that the same logical types of error, the same ways of going wrong, apply also to other emotional areas: the area of sex, choosing jobs, various types of personal relations, and so forth.

Before concluding this Part I should like to stress that investigation of the reason or unreason of various religions, whether by each individual or in some educational form, should not be too severely dissociated from the emotions in general. For any one person is likely to make the same *kind* of mistakes in *other* areas of his emotional life; and these mistakes, together with the person's general psychological make-up, will connect closely with the sort of religion he has – we cannot well tackle the one without the other.

Further, although we have concentrated on what is logically essential to the concept of religion – namely, awe and worship – it need hardly be said that many *other* emotions come into most actual religions. Various faiths purport to tell us what we should fear, feel guilty about, be proud of, reverent towards, and so forth: they claim to give us a general guide to the emotions and their appropriate objects. So investigation of these religions will necessarily involve the emotions in general, not just awe. We may, of course, study actual religions in their other aspects – their history, their claims to factual knowledge, their institutional practices their morality and so forth. But insofar as we are seriously interested in the reasonableness of religion, it is on the area of the emotions that our attention will always be focused. And there is a great deal of work to be done here, since there are many emotions, all of which need careful study and understanding: I have not here had space even to begin this task. It seems to me that we are only standing on the threshold of serious inquiry: all I hope to have done is to point the way that such inquiry should take.

six

Some Approaches

IN PART I we tried to pin down what was essential or peculiar to religion as a human activity, and found this to lie somewhere in the area of *awe* and *worship*. If a Martian came to earth and was trying to make sense of what he saw going on in Christian churches, Buddhist meetings, Mohammedan temples and so on, he would have to understand what it was to *worship* someone or something – otherwise he could not make sense of it at all: to him these would just be social gatherings or clubs, or groups of people who told stories (myths) or people who had a common morality.

We are dealing, then, with people who have various 'pictures', as I shall call them, of the world which include things or entities that are to be worshipped: this is what makes them *religious* pictures. Christians, for instance, have a picture which is painted in terms of a single God (consisting of three persons, 'Father', 'Son' and 'Holy Spirit'), who created and sustains the universe, who sent his son to earth as Jesus Christ, who forgives sins, and so on: there is an after life, the possibility of praying to God and being answered, a number of saints (and the Virgin Mary, mother of Jesus) who are to be worshipped or at least revered, and a Church (or churches) which is directed by God. Attached to this picture, or (if you like) part of it, there are certain specific moral principles (the Ten Commandments, a particular view of sexual morality), certain rituals (the Mass or Communion service), and – as it has historically happened – certain characteristic forms of art, literature and music: the psalms, the Gothic cathedrals, Bach's masses and cantatas. All these social and artistic attachments *celebrate*, or express, or reinforce, the basic Christian picture.

Of course there is not only one 'Christian picture' but many – the Roman Catholic, the Greek Orthodox, the Protestant, the Baptist and so on. Equally there are an enormous number of other 'pictures' which are not Christian at all. Not only are there the so-called 'higher' religions – Mohammedanism, Buddhism, Hinduism, Judaism – but there are innumerable others in the long history of man: various types of religion common among the ancient Greeks and Romans; primitive religions in which men appeared to worship animals, totems, little gods and spirits; 'state' religions like Fascism or those common in the Roman Empire, in which a dictator or emperor was worshipped as a god; and many pictures which are at least semi-religious, such as the creeds of the Stoics or the Marxists.

In this part of the book we want to say something about these and other religions (faiths, creeds, pictures); and in view of their enormous number and variety, it is clear that we shall not be able to say very much. But we ought at least to begin by considering the general question '*How* can we study or learn about these religious pictures?' or 'What sort of approach are we to adopt, if we want to make sense of this bewildering variety?' There is indeed an established subject, known as 'Comparative Religion', whose business it is to do this; but it is not all clear how this subject is best handled. Should we, for instance, plunge straight into the sacred writings of the religions – the Bible, the Koran, the writings of Buddha or the ancient Greeks? Or should we watch Christians and Buddhists when they are actually worshipping? Or when they are making moral decisions? Or ought we rather to study the history of the Christian church, or the Roman Empire?

There is no single 'right answer' to this question, because how you study something depends very much on your own particular interests and purposes. To take a simple and in a way a rather silly example, if you are concerned only with giving a lunch or a dinner-party which will not offend your guests, then all you need to know about Judaism and Hinduism is that some Jews will not eat pork and some Hindus will not eat beef. If you are an emperor or a general fighting a war, you need to know that certain Christians may be pacifists, or that you can't move Sikh troops across the water without trouble, because crossing water is against their religion. Politicians may know that Roman Catholic voters will be unlikely to vote for Communist candidates. Seducers might work out that Mohammedan girls are very chaste and not likely to yield to their advances. And so on.

I think most people would agree that this kind of interest is not an interest in *the religion in itself*. Such a person would not be concerned with the religion, but only with how it affected his own ends. Concern of this kind is not disreputable, but it is not very serious. Moreover, it is in fact very difficult to predict the behaviour and reactions of religious believers unless you do take their belief seriously, and on its own terms: that is, unless you try to 'get the feel of' or 'get inside' a religion. This seems to me to be the guiding principle for the study of religions. The key questions are 'What is it *like to be* a Christian (Buddhist, ancient Greek, etc.)?', 'Just what *is* the Christian picture, and why do Christians have it?', and 'What are the underlying forces which make this picture what it is?'

Apart from hostesses, generals, politicians and seducers there are of course plenty of serious scholars who study religion from various points of view. These points of view or approaches can be listed briefly:

1. The *history* of religion: how did it come about that Mohammed had such success in spreading his beliefs? What happened to the Christian church when it became the official religion of the Roman Empire?

2. The *sociology* of religion: how did the religion of ancient Egypt reinforce the Pharaoh and the system of government? What is the connection between the Protestant movement and the development of trade by the middle-classes?

3. The '*history of ideas*' in religions: how did the sayings of Jesus become part of an official body of doctrine in Christianity? Did the ancient Greeks come to see Zeus as the one supreme god?

4. The *anthropology* of religion: how do the rituals of worshipping the Greek Artemis compare with those of worshipping the Virgin Mary? Why do certain tribes have witch-doctors, and what are their powers and functions in the tribes?

5. The *psychology* of religion: what forces are there in individual

people which connect religion with sex? Why do some peoples
worship a father-god, and others a mother-goddess?

These five approaches are not anything like as distinct as I have
made them sound; it is fairly obvious that they interconnect and
overlap. Indeed one of the most important things in studying any
religion is to appreciate the *variety* of causes and factors which
make a religion what it is. To take an (over-simplified) example:
we could say that the rise of the Protestant movement in Europe,
from Luther onwards, came about in a way that demands our
attention to all the five approaches. First, the history of the times:
perhaps the abuses of the Roman Catholic Church, and the desire
of north European cities for independence, was bound to lead to a
split. Second, a new social class – the merchant middle-class – was
becoming stronger in north Europe, and the Protestant morality
with its emphasis on thrift and individual conscience suited that
class. Third, the study of existing Christian doctrine led (or so at
least it seemed to Luther) to further inevitable conclusions: Christian ideas were moving towards Protestant belief. Fourth, the kind
of independent, anti-authoritarian set-up characteristic of Protestantism, with less emphasis on images and pictures and remote,
'magical' priests, and more involvement on the part of the con-
gregation, suited the more democratic and independent-minded
people of the time. Fifth, the vigour of these people enabled them
to support the strain of using their own individual consciences,
backed by the Bible, to make up their minds: they no longer
needed so much guidance from external authority in the form of
the Pope and the priesthood.

I do not want to say that any of these suggestions are correct:
the point is that all of them are *possible*, and this means that we
cannot afford to neglect any of the five approaches mentioned
above. Clearly these five types of factor would interact with and
reinforce each other; and we should only achieve any real understanding by a very prolonged and detailed examination of
Luther's Germany and other areas. Moreover, we should have to
look at other things as well: for instance, the *spirit* of Protestantism
does not appear only in its doctrines or rituals, but in (say) the
cantatas of Bach or the writings of Calvin. A proper appreciation

of Bach's canata 'Ein Feste Burg' gives us the sort of four-square, independent, salvationist 'feel' of Protestantism more truly than many other things do; just as an appreciation of the words and style of the Collects and the Authorized Version of the Bible gives us the 'feel' of the Church of England.

It is for this reason that I want to concentrate particularly, in what follows, on the fifth approach: that is, the psychological. For there is a clear sense in which this is – not the most important, for all are important – but the most immediately central and relevant to the spirit that informs particular religions, to the 'feel' of them, and hence to an understanding of the 'picture' which the religion consists of. As we saw in Part I, religion is centrally concerned with the emotions – perhaps in particular with the unconscious emotions: it is what a person or group *does with* his feelings of awe, guilt, reverence, fear, desire for life and strength, and so on, that determines what sort of religion he has. These are the paints or colouring-matter for his picture.

Again, this is not to say that other factors are irrelevant, and perhaps an example will show both their relevance and also the centrality of psychology. An account (again over-simplified) of the rise of Hitler-worship would obviously have to take account of the historical and sociological position of Germany in the 1920s and 1930s: indeed, we might have to go back to the rise of Prussia in the 19th century in order to understand certain things about the Germans. The chaos in financial and economic life, the unemployment, the feelings of resentment and injustice against the nations who had won the 1914–18 war – all these are relevant to Hitler's rise to power. But when we inspect the religion that grew up around him, we are forced to think in psychological terms. We have the anxiety, the sense of hopelessness, the loss of purpose and personal identity, which led many people to put their hopes into what was, in effect, a 'supernatural' or mythical 'other world': a world in which Germany was triumphant, into which they were led by a hero or god, Adolf Hitler, who was destined to conquer and endowed with supernatural qualities of foresight, wisdom, strength, knowledge and glory. There were 'devils', the Jews and the eastern Slav (non-Aryan) peoples, who were trying to poison the purity of the German nation and drag it down, and who hence had to be persecuted, or massacred, or invaded. 'Goodness' meant obedience to the Führer, and his orders: piety and devotion meant attending the party rallies, giving the Fascist salute, reading and believing the words of the Führer, and working for the state. The 'hymn' was *Deutschland über alles,* Germany over all.

This was a religion, because so much of the emotion of many Germans was involved in it, to the point of worship. Other nations are patriotic, and some perhaps maintain a similar fervour (consider talk about 'Arab destiny', 'Mother Russia', and other such cases); but there are few cases so clear-cut. What has happened is this: certain very central, and in a way very *ordinary*, human emotions, become focused on a particular individual (Hitler) and a particular picture of life (Nazism). We all, sometimes, want a hero or a god: feel hopeless or despondent: want to identify ourselves with a triumphant cause: find decision-making too anxious or difficult, so resign ourselves gratefully to the orders of other people who seem stronger than ourselves: feel threatened or poisoned by some 'impure' element, often connected with race or sex, which arouses our alarm and hence our anger against what we see as 'alien', 'different', or 'disgusting'. These and other emotions are *dressed up*, so to speak, in a particular set of religious clothes: in this case, Nazi clothes. As a result of this dressing-up, there follow religious rituals, doctrines, hymns and so on.

Other approaches have a lot to tell us about why the dressing-up goes on in the way it does: psychology tells us something of *what is underneath the clothes*. For it is fairly clear that, though religions differ very greatly, they nevertheless deal with much the same emotions, emotions which are common to all human beings – even if some are suppressed and others on the surface. Awe, guilt, purity, a sense of purpose – these and others are as it were the *stuff* of religion. For instance, the existence of sexuality in human beings generates intense desire, dread, guilt, passion and feelings of magic power. One religion (the worship of Cybele) may have a ritual in which priests castrate themselves in a state of maddened frenzy: another may lay down very stringent rules against sexual behaviour, as we find in Leviticus and the writings of St Jerome: another may celebrate fertility and the sexual act, as we induce from the statues and offerings of primitive peoples and (sometimes) from Indian writings like the *Kama Sutra*: and there will be many other variations. But all these try to *deal with* these sexual emotions, to give them a framework, a set of rituals and rules and institutions which will accommodate them and make it easier for the individual to cope with them. So too with the other emotions.

It is perhaps worth noting here that, in this respect, religion undertakes a task which cannot be avoided. Since the emotions are present in all of us, we have to deal with them somehow: to give them a form, a structure, a set of clothes. It is not strictly necessary that the structure should be 'religious' in the precise sense of involving awe and worship; but in a wider sense, every man is bound to have some kind of structure or system which accommodates his emotions. Whether we call this a 'value system', 'creed', 'way of life', 'set of principles', 'set of preferences', 'philosophy of life' or whatever, it is inevitable. The study of religion, and of 'philosophies' or 'creeds' which we may not want to call strictly religious, is the study of how men and groups of men have tried to come to terms with their emotions and the world, and to give them some shape.

I do not want to convey the impression that men, or groups of men, consciously and deliberately worked out for themselves what structure or shape to give to their feelings. In many cases men have simply taken over the structure – the religion – that their fathers had: they have been brought up to believe it, find (perhaps) that it works reasonably well for them, and just carry on. In other cases, where they have more than one religion to choose from, they instinctively or automatically fly into the arms of whatever creed or faith offers them the kind of psychological support and structure they need – and this is not so much to *choose* a religion as to be *drawn towards* it. People find themselves moving like sleepwalkers, 'drifting' towards Communism, or 'coming nearer' to the Catholic Church, or 'feeling in sympathy' with the Buddhists. This is what usually happens.

But it is plainly possible to develop more powers of choice in ourselves: to give ourselves some chance of being reasonable in our selection of a religion or a 'way of life', along the lines mentioned in Part I. This gives the study of religion a practical importance: it is not merely something which happens to interest historians and sociologists. For if we are to become more reasonable, we need first to *understand* other religions from a psychological point of view: to gain some insight into the ways in which men have structured their emotions. We can and must do this, at least to begin with, from a neutral point of view: that is, without too quickly condemning particular structures (religions) as unreasonable. Thus to most of us it may seem that the worship of Hitler was quite insane, irrelevant to our own life, indeed incomprehensible. But (as I hope our example showed) the emotions which the Germans felt were emotions which are in all of us: they are comprehensible enough if we have the patience and insight to look at them, and relevant enough if we can work out how we ourselves structure them.

What I am going to do in the rest of this Part, then, is to take a look at some instances of religious belief, and try to see what sort of emotions are operating. This will involve us also in sidelong glances at the sociological and historical background of the belief; but I shall not be spending a great deal of time on this. Most books on comparative religion – and there are many good ones, some of which I have mentioned in the bibliography – deal in turn with at least the 'major' or 'higher' religions; and if you are particularly interested in a general or complete view of the various religions, I should advise you to read one or more of them – not forgetting that there is still some tendency to underplay the primitive or less 'respectable' religions in such books, a tendency you can compensate for by reading some anthropology of primitive religions. I do not want to compete with books of that kind: I have neither the ability nor the space. But I think that, by the study of one or two examples, we can at least get some idea of how to approach different religions, and some notion of the major emotions that underlie them.

In doing this it is important to avoid one major error. We often talk of religious 'belief' as if it were like other kinds of belief: as if for instance, 'There is a God' were like 'There is life on other planets' or 'There are sharks in the Mediterranean'. Most belief is arrived at by considering *evidence*, being guided by the facts, and reaching a conclusion. But religious belief is not like that. As we have said, it is more like a picture to which a person is emotionally wedded: to which he is attached, not by evidence, but by his feelings (such a person may use words like 'faith', 'revelation', or 'commitment' here). It is none the worse for that; but this means that we must, in our study of religions, lay aside for the time being the question of whether these pictures are 'true'. They are not meant to be true: not, at least, in the sense in which we think it is true that the earth goes round the sun, or that three angles of a triangle add up to 180 degrees.

I mention this because, in many books written about religion, you will find that the authors are partisan. In our society, for instance, the author may well be adopting a Christian viewpoint; and such a person will naturally see the other religions as better or worse approximations to Christianity. In Communist countries authors may see all religion as a wicked device to enslave the working classes. If we *start* with the idea that some religions are 'right' or 'true', we shall inevitably distort both them and the others, and limit our understanding of them. We have to take them for what they are: very much as a psychoanalyst takes his patients for what they are, without praising or judging or condemning them, but just trying to understand how their minds work. It is only much later, armed with whatever insight we manage to get into other people and ourselves, that we can start to evaluate religions in terms of 'being reasonable'.

seven

Jews, Greeks and Romans

THE ANCIENT civilizations of the Jews, Greeks and Romans provide us with quite a good focus of attention for several reasons. In particular (1) they give us a very wide variety of religious types, and (2) they offer far more examples of primitive religious elements than we can easily gain from (for instance) modern versions of Christianity: indeed, in these early civilizations it is possible to trace the development of primitive taboos and local cults into a more complex and sophisticated religious structure. We shall begin by saying something about the latter.

Local gods and taboos
In primitive cultures, disconnected from each other by bad communications and hostility, we expect to find different gods worshipped in different ways under different names. This is what we find in Greece and Rome; and, though the ways in which the Jews handled this situation were not the ways of the Greeks and Romans, we find the same in ancient Palestine.

These local gods naturally represented the particular local interests of the cultures. Many of these were concerned with agriculture: thus in early Roman religion we can trace 'the god of corn-disease', and other (to us) petty deities concerned with hearth and home ('household gods', the Lares and Penates). In Greece gods would be associated with particular animals and localities (Mount Olympus), and in Palestine there were the competing rivalries of Baal, Dagon and other local objects of worship. Each of these had their own names, their own particular rituals and associations.

The Greek and Roman peoples were invaded and dominated by Aryan-speaking tribes from north-east Europe who brought a new religion with them – the Olympian gods like the Greek Zeus and the Roman Jupiter (= Zeus + pater, 'skyfather'), Artemis/Diana, Aphrodite/Venus, Pallas Athene and others. These names persisted, and we are familiar with the gods of classical literature, first codified by Homer, and continuing until Christianity became the official religion of the Roman Empire. But the actual religion of the Greeks and Romans was an intricate blend of this new 'Olympian' picture with the innumerable local cults. Briefly, they did not destroy or outlaw these cults, but came to terms with them. Thus Pausanias describes the worship of Zeus or Artemis as being practised differently in different places; and these gods have, as it were, local names in addition to their own – 'Zeus of Hymettus', 'Artemis of Brauron', and so on. It is as if the local deities at Hymettus and Brauron had been rechristened: a great deal of the old worship was incorporated in the new.

This left considerable scope for variation in religious practice among individuals and local townships; and among such practices and rituals many traditional taboos or superstitions survived. Certainly few were outlawed. Moreover, although of course when major cities developed (Athens, Rome) the 'centre of worship' would naturally be in such cities, there would be a good deal of religious decentralization. Nowhere would be *the* (only) temple, *the* sacred shrine, *the* place of power and seat of worship.

By contrast, the Jews first developed a clear picture of their own God (Jehovah) as *the* (only true) god who ought to be worshipped by all peoples, and then spent a good deal of their history in keeping themselves and their god sharply dissociated from other peoples and gods. Even when they conquered, they did not accommodate or assimilate (or at least, they always professed not to have done), but simply obliterated competing deities and rituals. As we shall see, there are many aspects to this remarkable and uncompromising monotheism, which incidentally shares many features with Mohammedanism; but one aspect is the enormous *centralization* of religion which it entailed. The Temple, the Law, the very identity of the Jews themselves were all defined by it – as well as a clearly-defined priesthood which has no real parallel in Greece and Rome.

I will not try to account for this striking development in terms of the Jews' social structure, the climate and geographical conditions under which they lived, and other such factors. But it is obvious that very different, or at least differently-structured, emotions were involved. In particular this centralization, the insistence on *one god* ('and we are his people'), went along with very detailed and restricted taboos which, like the centralization, are essentially concerned with *purity*. The endless injunctions in Leviticus and Deuteronomy concern not only obvious social rules against murder and theft, but a remarkable series of commands concerning what may and may not be eaten, and about sexual behaviour. It is as if the 'higher' (if we may so call it) conception of God could only be gained at a price; the price of constant vigilance in the face of the temptations of the flesh.

By contrast, there is not much that is austere (though much that is magnificent) in Greek and Roman religion. There the sexual and food taboos are very mild, and (as we shall see) the connection with morality very much weaker than with the Jews. If the Greek and Roman gods are noble, it is not with the severe and stark nobility of the Jewish Jehovah. To some temperaments the former religion will seem weak, pleasure-loving, more suitable for art and literature than for the belief of a serious-minded and virtuous man. To others the Jewish creed seems over-harsh, inflexible, unwilling to accept the various forces and powers in the world and in man for what they are.

The fear of corruption, of losing racial and moral purity, is something that we all feel and – in some degree – ought perhaps to feel. *Some* concept of purity, fidelity, integrity is necessary. If a religious picture is to accommodate *everything*, it no longer has a character of its own: indeed it is no longer intelligible as a picture, since 'anything goes'. (Just as one may have various concepts of 'faithfulness' in marriage – and these may include the traditional Christian monogamy, or the fidelity of many wives to a single husband, or almost anything: but there if there is *no* limit, if 'anything goes', then the notion of marriage disappears altogether.) The Jews had a very 'tight' or narrow concept of purity in religion, and hence in their lives generally: the Greeks and Romans a very accommodating one.

E

Mothers, fathers and icons

The same contrast between Greco-Roman 'permissiveness' and Jewish severity emerges in a psychologically very interesting phenomenon – the ban on any kind of pictorial representation ('icon') of the Jewish God: no statues, no paintings, carvings, bas-reliefs, black-and-white drawings or anything of that kind at all. In Greece and Rome, on the other hand, there were innumerable representations of the gods; not only in the temple-statues, but as a common subject-matter for everyday objects, such as common Greek pottery.

The Jews share this peculiarity with the Mohammedans, and there seems to be a connection between it and the worship of a remote father-god. Jehovah, we might say, is more *inhuman* than the Greek gods. If he is associated with anything, it is with the notion of *commandments* and *language,* not with any physical presence – and certainly not with the sometimes voluptuous representations of Greco-Roman painting and statuary. Jehovah was isolated, on his own, the great I AM, the Word that was in the beginning. He is a highly abstracted force, creator and commander.

By contrast, Greco-Roman religion was not only polytheistic but – at least as important psychologically – a combination of the worship of both male and female deities. This is not, or not only, to be explained by the position of women, which in most of Greek and Roman history was as 'inferior' as among the Jews. It is as if the Jews, by a herculean psychological effort, deliberately turned themselves against everything that we associate with the 'feminine': against the physical (particularly the sexual), the gracious and the beautiful. This is not to say that they were immune from such feelings, as the Song of Solomon shows clearly enough: but they were, so to speak, officially disowned. Most Jewish art appears in *verbal* form; the Old Testament is at once law, morality, religious doctrine, history and poetry.

The same contrast repeats itself in the history of Christianity, in which the worship or near-worship of the Virgin Mary at once took account of the 'feminine' forces of man's nature and attempted to 'spiritualize' them. Yet the statues, the paintings, the colours, the dangerous-seeming beauty of much Christian practice was utterly rejected by the Puritan movement in England. It was not only, nor even chiefly, for reasons of doctrine and logic that Cromwell's party destroyed so much that was beautiful in English churches. Representations of any kind – including any sort of *acting* or *pretence* – seemed immoral and threatening to the purity of the believer.

It is as if the Jews and Puritans felt their spiritual integrity to be very much at the mercy of these 'feminine' feelings, and needed to have a father-god in the sharpest possible contrast with them. He had to be *one* (the only) god, for even diversity was alarming. He had to be male, because (in almost all societies) the father gives the orders, and the mother the comfort, the physical pleasure, the physical warmth: indeed, whatever the society, only the mother can give the child his first experience of pleasure and satisfied desire at her breast.

The Greeks and Romans, one might say, took much more account of the variety of human need and desire. At times, as in the plays of Aeschylus, there is an attempt to reach out towards Zeus as the one supreme god; but he was never the sole creator of the world, and behind Zeus always stood the Fates, or grim Necessity. And, whatever the philosophers of the time might say, there was Apollo, Artemis, Poseidon, Athene, Aphrodite and a host of others to represent all aspects of human experience. In Euripides' *Hippolytus* the hero is caught between two conflicting forces – chastity, represented by Artemis, and sexual passion, represented by Aphrodite. Both were valid, both powerful, both to be respected.

Morality and Power

As we might expect, there is a similar contrast in the relationship between religion and morality. Jehovah was, in a sense, morality incarnate: he is identifiable primarily as a source of moral injunction. He gives the Ten Commandments, punishes the wicked and rewards the virtuous: he can do no wrong – by definition, for right and wrong are defined in terms of his will. Not so with the Greco-Roman gods. There is no indication that their will was thought to be *morally good*.

The Greco-Roman gods are powerful, and it is wisest to obey

them, because otherwise a man gets into trouble. Entertain strangers, because a stranger may be Zeus in disguise: sacrifice to Poseidon, otherwise you may suffer shipwreck: respect Aphrodite, otherwise you may be the victim of uncontrollable sexual passion. But, apart from anything else, there are many gods, and they take sides: some are for the Greeks, others for the Trojans – it is a question of whose will prevails, not whose will is the most righteous.

It is only in the 'state religion', the emperor-worship of the Roman Empire, that the connection between morality and worship is made: and even then it is a far cry from the Jewish religion, though this was also the official worship of the Jewish state. In Rome, it was politically desirable that the various peoples in the Empire should unite in some common bond of religious loyalty; and so it became obligatory for loyal citizens to show this by referring to the emperor as 'a god' or 'divine' (*divus*) and burning a pinch of incense on his altar. But no more than this: the bond was a very loose one. A citizen could have other religions besides this: indeed it was hardly a serious religion at all – not much more, perhaps, than agreeing to stand up and sing 'God Save the Queen'.

The fact that the Jews (and early Christians), almost alone of all the peoples in the Empire, refused to comply with this minimal requirement is itself significant. To them, it *mattered* whether one even called the emperor 'divine': for to them, there was only one god, and it was dangerously sacrilegious and blasphemous to play with fire. The Jewish state, the Jewish people, did not believe in Jehovah as any kind of political symbol, a god who conveniently served the cause of social unity (though Jehovah did do this): they believed in him because he was real to them as the Roman emperors were never real to the peoples of the Empire. To the Romans, emperor-worship was not much more than a kind of baptism of the official order and the establishment. A critic once described the Church of England as 'the Tory Party at prayer': that is not far from the mark as a parallel with Rome.

Salvation and the after life
It is remarkable that, on the surface at least, the official beliefs of both the Greco-Roman and the Jewish world gave the believer no

serious hope of life after death. True, the Jewish dead may have had a shadowy existence in 'Sheol', and the Greeks and Romans in the underworld of Hades; but it was clear that this was, at least, a very inferior kind of life.

However, religious beliefs that promised more to the believer were popular in the Greco-Roman world, even if not officially countenanced, well before the rise of Christianity. The Eleusinian mysteries, the rites of Isis and the hope of Mithras all bear witness to this. Interestingly, the concept of entering on life after death goes hand in hand with the concept of salvation: of some kind of purification, usually involving baptism and secret initiation rites, which will somehow free the believer from the evils of this world and enable him to enter the next. (The religion of ancient Egypt is a well-documented case.)

There is a certain nobility in the acceptance of death in the official creeds. 'A short and irrecoverable time is the life of all men: but to extend one's fame by deeds – this is the toil, this the task' says Aeneas in Vergil: and Homer's Achilles admits that, even though king among the dead, he had rather be a mere serf, tilling the fields for a harsh master, but alive and seeing the light of the sun. When Catullus says that 'suns may set and rise again but we, when once our sun is set, must sleep one long unending night', he uses it as an argument for making merry while the sun shines; but equally for other writers it was an argument for noble deeds, for leaving a name and memorial behind one.

But this was not enough for most men; and the salvationist, life-after-death religions became increasingly popular. Christianity was one of these; and part of its success – it has had a longer run than any other religion – was its ability to cater for almost the whole variety of human desires. It promised, via a saviour, eternal life; at the same time, it retained the concept of a remote father-figure who must be obeyed. By skilful, if unconscious, use of male and female figures (the saints and Virgin) it allowed for a variety of worship-objects; yet there was a moral code too. Perhaps the chief attraction was a well worked out concept of heaven, attached to the moral code, but filled also with the beauties experienced on earth, which could be achieved even by the humblest and most oppressed citizen.

It is obvious that the fear of death is one of the deepest human feelings. This fear, and the corresponding desire for continuation of the self in one form or other, lies at the root of much human endeavour: the creation of buildings and empires and works of art, the desire for children, the need to be remembered. Most successful religions cater for this fear in one form or another – by the hope of reincarnation, the attainment of heaven, or some other device. Nevertheless, the Jewish and the Greco-Roman faiths show that it is at least possible – even if a desolating experience – to face the possibility that this world is all, and still to live as a human being. There is a tone of underlying sadness which is apparent in the Jewish writings (in the Psalms, for instance) as well as in the literature of Greece and Rome; a tone very different from the secret, half-furtive and half-ecstatic rituals of the salvationist religions such as Isis-worship or Mithraism.

In this chapter we have done no more than point to a few themes which are, in one form or another, common to most religions: monotheism, the nature of taboos, purity, the male and female element in deities, the connection with morality, and life after death. I have not attempted to do justice to even small aspects of the actual religions of Greece, Rome and Palestine. But the reader should now, at least, be better able to trace out these themes there for himself by wider reading: or, if he prefers, to trace them in other religions. Mohammedanism, for instance, makes a useful comparison: a sort of extreme version, one might say, of the Judaeo–Christian religion. Or we may contrast the polytheism of the Hindus with Greek polytheism: the Norse myths and worship of Wotan with the early worship of Zeus. Or, again, we may try to see the origins of these faiths in primitive religions, beyond the scope of written history, but none the less important for that. I leave it to the reader to decide in what direction he will go by himself.

eight

Religions and 'Philosophies'

In this chapter I want to look briefly at a class of outlooks or 'philosophies' which may take a religious form (in the strict sense of involving awe and worship), but which are in a sense more sophisticated and less 'primitive' than the Jewish and Greco–Roman beliefs we looked at in the last chapter. Perhaps we may express the difference roughly like this: For simple-minded people, their religion (whatever it was) was not a sophisticated or 'abstract' thing, and did not necessarily involve anything we could call a 'philosophy of life', nor any high-level generalizations about 'how to live'. To a naïve peasant, Zeus might virtually *be* the statue in the temple, or the Virgin Mary *be* her image in the local church. He would have his local saints, his local priest, his particular prayers connected with his everyday life, his simple-minded picture of 'heaven' or 'hell'. Other more sophisticated people, whether in ancient Athens or a modern city, would not be content with this: something like a theology or a philosophy of religion would appear, less obviously and immediately connected with the emotions, and dressed up in much more 'abstract' and 'intellectual' clothes.

Note that both these people may have shared in a sense, the same religion or outlook. Both the simple peasant and the professor of theology may call themselves Christians; or to take another example, it is possible to be 'stoical' in a simple way, or to make a 'philosophy' out of it (Stoicism). Again, one may join the Communist Party in the role of a naïve worker and fighter, or one may be more theoretical and adopt Communism or Marxism as a general way of life. Most religions have had people of both kinds. In Hinduism, for instance, we find not only historical changes in religious belief, but beliefs which are quite different (or at least on a different level of sophistication) held by different Hindus at the same period of history. To one the gods Vishnu, Shiva, Krishna and others may be taken as 'real people', separate and distinct forces in the world: to another, more theoretically inclined, they may be regarded as 'different aspects of reality'. So too, to one Roman, Mars and Apollo and Jupiter may be thought of as actual entities living in the sky: to another, they may be little more than personifications of natural phenomena (rather as we might talk of 'Cupid', meaning no more than 'love').

At this more sophisticated level, people make some attempt to solve the large-scale problems of life, of being in the world, by producing a 'philosophy'. This 'philosophy' may draw on a particular religious tradition, but will not necessarily be confined by it. For example, there are Christians nowadays who live (or think they ought to live) by a 'philosophy' which is conceived basically in terms of love, concern for others, the importance of peace and social service and racial integration and brotherhood, and so on. As Christians, they will quote (we might say, *use*) the words of Jesus and examples of Christian saints to support this; but their actual 'working' philosophy, in this respect anyway, may be no different from some humanists who have the same outlook.

These philosophies may serve many different purposes; but the purpose I want to consider here concerns the provision of a psychological security in a harsh world. As we have seen, there have been many cases where this problem was solved by believing in another world (heaven, a reincarnation) which gave the required feeling of security: if this world was harsh, that did not matter much, since soon we shall enter the next. But, except in a few of these cases, this belief was insufficient. However skilfully the next world was depicted – and mediaeval Christian writers, to name but one example, put a lot of effort into such pictures – it rarely seemed *real* enough to solve the problem. Some picture or philosophy was required to make *this* world tolerable.

What, in general, is intolerable about it? We might say, it is that we have desires of various kinds – for health, riches, happiness, and so on – which are very often frustrated. To want things is to be at risk, for we may not get them: and there follows disappointment, anger, despair. (This is easily visible in young children,

and persists into adult life.) What picture, what philosophy, will
help us to 'grow up', or at least to pretend that we have grown up?
What will make our own frustrations tolerable, or help us to avoid
frustration? I shall outline five general approaches to this problem.

1. *Buddhism and the abolition of desire*
One way of solving the problem of frustrated desires is – to abandon the desires. This solution emerges most clearly in certain
Buddhist doctrines. The attainment of Nirvana, in which the individual soul merges with a cosmos as 'a drop of water with the
shining sea', involves the abolition of desire together with the abolition of the self. Much Buddhist practice was concerned with the
freeing of the self from various objects of affection and interest in
this world; indeed we should learn to regard this world as in a way
illusory, unreal, an improper object of desire. We must rise above
it, learn to do without it.

   This approach is not confined to Buddhism. It appears, in a way
in Plato's *Republic*, where we are told that only the 'Ideal Forms'
of things are real, and what we take as reality is only a shadow.
The Christian 'Not my will, but thine' involves a similar abandon-
ment of the self: though there it is rather a matter of being completely dependent on another, the father-figure who will guide
one's steps aright. Other religions of the East, some of which were
connected with Buddhism (Taoism, Confucianism), also stress this
approach.

   In more modern terms, we can detect this way of solving the
problem in many individuals and social groups. If life is hard, the
answer is – not to care. This may involve a willingness to submerge
the self completely: not to submerge it *in* anything, as a Communist submerges it in his Party or a pleasure-seeker in his pleasures,
but simply to escape from the self altogether. The taking of drugs
can, obviously enough, be used for this purpose. The world is
unpleasant: very well, we can enter a new world under the
influence of drugs in which the whole business of desire and
achievement, success and failure, the whole apparatus of con-
sciousness, is either obliterated or at least much diminished. It
makes little difference whether we describe such states of mind as

'mystical', 'dreaming', 'doped', or whatever. The effect is the same.

2. Stoicism and self-sufficiency

Another way of solving the problem, though similar in some respects, emerges in the Stoic ideal, which first became popular in the Roman Empire. If we conceive of life as a troubled and stormy sea, we can say that the Buddhist approach was (in the last resort) to abandon the self entirely, to merge with the sea. The Stoic approach is to make oneself into an immovable rock, which the waves buffet in vain.

This involves drawing a sharp distinction between the self and the objects surrounding the self. One Stoic suggests that we learn to do without these objects by a process of training in 'self-sufficiency': we must get used to our precious crockery being broken, then to our pet dog dying, finally even to the illness and death of our wives and children. Our inner selves should remain untouched: the rock is unmoved, but at the cost of dissociating itself from the attachment to the earth and sand and other things that surround it.

To the Stoics the self was *important* (here is the contrast with some Buddhist writings). In each man was 'a particle of the divine gold', something like a *soul,* which could not be swept away whatever happened in the outside world. The soul participated in the spirit of the universe, the 'mind' which was everywhere. It was a fortress in itself, needing no outside help from god or man. A man was, perhaps, bound to have desires; but he should learn to be (or at least to appear) unmoved if they were not fulfilled. He should not, so to speak, bet on them, but on himself.

This too is an ideal which we can see some people adopting in more modern times. The unconquerable hero who loses everything, gets beaten up, is abused and hated, but nevertheless retains his identity and is 'true to himself', has a great attraction for us – in thrillers and detective stories as well as in real life. The 'tough guy' hero is not only tough to others, but tough in himself: he can 'take it'. The price paid is dissociation from other people, some severance of the bonds of natural affection. But his integrity is preserved – almost, we might say, his *purity.*

3. Epicureanism and common-sense

A quite different approach was adopted by the Greek Epicurus and his followers. Instead of trying to make yourself into an immovable rock amid a sea of troubles, you should rather adjust and accommodate yourself to the waves, like a buoy or a canoe, rising and falling with them. Instead of 'taking life on the chin', like a boxer who will not give ground, you should 'roll with the punch', bowing graciously to the inevitable. Take pleasure where you find it; remember that this life is all we have: accept fate, change and chance.

In many ways this seems a sane and attractive doctrine; but somehow it never managed to inspire the hearts of men. For one thing, it involved a kind of atheism (Epicurus thought that if there were gods, they did not concern themselves with men) and a rejection of the after life. But this lack is perhaps only a symptom of a more general deficiency: the failure to give people any hope of *salvation*, even in this world. The other four approaches we are considering all make some attempt at this: they enable people to look forward, if not to an after life, at any rate to *something* – or at least, they give people a 'high ideal', an inspiration, to cling to: something 'other-worldly', if not actually in another world.

Whether or not this approach ought to be enough for people, it did not seem enough. In the Buddhist approach, we are told that we really ought not to bet on life at all: it is ultimately better to resign from the game. In the Stoic, we are told to bet only on ourselves. In the Epicurean, we are to hedge our bets: we must not commit ourselves too much to any *one* thing. We must not put all our money on one girl to love, one job to get; we must take things as they come, deriving a mild and moderate pleasure from what the fates grant us, and hence avoiding disappointment if we are sometimes unsuccessful – rather as wise investors or business-men 'diversify' their resources, rather than putting all their money into some one product or industry. When the party of life is over, we should get up and go graciously. All this has a certain sophisticated charm: but the desires and fears of most people were too strong for such an approach to satisfy them.

4. *Communism and heaven on earth*

Quite different again are the philosophies, of which Communism is in our day a clear example, which (as it were) do not accept the terms of the problem. We are not just to take it for granted that life is difficult, frustrating, and unsatisfying: we are not to resign ourselves to despair, or try to be self-sufficient and immovable, or adjust ourselves graciously to circumstances. We ought rather to adjust circumstances to ourselves. The frustrations of life are changeable: they are, perhaps, due wholly or largely to the wrong social or economic system (Capitalism, or the profit motive, or whatever). We can change this, and make all well.

This is a much more aggressive and attractive approach, at least to many people in an age when scientific progress and technology can in fact change many aspects of our lives for the better (or, of course, worse). We *can* get what we want, the message runs: nothing is impossible to us: even death may yield to medical science, and meanwhile the problems of hunger, envy, crime and mental illness can be solved by 'the new society'. We do not need, and must not rely on, external aids from supernatural or other sources. We need only the will to win, the belief in a better future, and faith in our own omnipotence.

Interestingly enough, however, Communist countries have either come to terms with the supernatural or created a religion of their own. Clearly, men like Lenin and Mao-Tse Tung are venerated somewhat as gods: there is a good deal of religious talk of 'the will of the Party', 'the ultimate classless society', and so on. There is (or was) to be a millenium, when all men would be brothers, free, happy, and united. Saviour-figures like Mao, lead us into this future. Alternatively, the state presses on with the pedestrian task of developing industry and raising the standard of living, while allowing the individuals, if they really must, to worship as Christians or Jews in privacy and without too much persecution. By one method or another the 'salvationist', 'other-worldly' element is retained. Even the Communists are, in fact, forced to accept the problem in its own terms. Life *is* frustrating, even under a truly socialist state. Perhaps indeed all that happens is that new *kinds* of frustration appear after a time: once the revolutionary fervour is over, life may indeed be in important respects better, but it still remains life: the 'wheel to which we are all bound', as a Buddhist writer puts it.

5. 'Honour' ethics

Finally an approach which has something in common with some of the others, but has also important differences. The desire for personal identity, for an enduring and satisfying sense of the self, can to some extent be assuaged by the pursuit of what we may call 'honour'. Certain aspects of Japanese religions, notably Bushido, have much to do with this concept; but it is a very common one, and not properly to be identified with any particular religious creed. It is, in effect, the desire to 'cut a figure', to be 'famous', to live up to a particular picture of oneself, to be an ideal type.

This can be thought of as a solution to the problem of life, because the business of living up to the ideal is not normally subject to the changes and chances of this world. To take a modern example, a sheriff can live up to his picture of an ideal sheriff – one who shows no fear of wicked gunfighters, who never backs down when challenged, who serves justice whatever the cost – whatever the circumstances. He may fail in achieving particular ends (say, to bring peace to a town in the West): but his real ends, what he really lives for, do not consist of *producing* anything, but simply of *being that sort of person*. And this he can do whatever happens. If he dies honourable and glorious, that is no loss to his ideal. It is not the results, but how he comports himself, that matters.

Stoicism can be seen, in a way, as a particular ideal of this kind; but 'honour' ethics vary widely as regards their content. Certain conduct and behaviour were required of a Homeric or Spartan hero: of a dignified Roman: of a mediaeval knight: of a Japanese samurai: of an English gentleman in the 18th century, and so on. But in all these cases there is a sort of aesthetic ideal of perfection. Women too, even in male-dominated societies (as most were and are), may have their ideals: the ideal of 'the perfect wife', 'the pure and innocent maiden', and so on.

It is essentially the *image* that counts here: and this approach is just as popular nowadays in modern society as it ever was. The desire to be 'with it', 'in the fashion': to establish one's identity in a harsh world by fitting oneself into a particular type, via clothes or hair-styles or success in the 'pop' world: these are the modern versions. The approach offers a solution, because anybody can do this just by *trying*. Instead of desiring what we may not get, we can make ourselves into the right sort of figure by (as it were) *acting* it consistently. So long as we go on acting we are safe from the blows of fate.

In this chapter, again, I have omitted much that is important. There are of course a great many other 'philosophies' than those mentioned, just as there are a great many other religions. But I hope to have shown that it is not just the 'primitive' religions – the ones some people might dismiss as 'superstition' or 'magic' – that are connected with human emotions. Much of the literature of Buddhism, Stoicism, Communism, etc. is extremely soph- isticated, just as much of the literature connected with Chris- tianity is extremely sophisticated. Complicated arguments have been constructed (like those in Aquinas or Marx), fine points of doctrine disputed, subtle considerations of logic put forward. But I think we can see – though we have not done justice to any 'philosophy' or religion – that underneath all this there is the desire to find some kind of *remedy*, to make life tolerable and to give our desires and needs some shape.

nine

Changes in Outlook

It is often difficult to identify with any precision the emotions and attitudes which underlie various religions and out-looks on life. One helpful device here, based on psychological research, is to analyse the *kinds of reasons* which religious people give for their beliefs, the general *style* or *mode of thought* which they use in their language and arguments. This will give us some clue about what is really going on 'underneath the surface', so to speak: a clue to what we may call the 'emotional logic' of the outlook.

There are four basic 'modes', which may be described briefly as follows:

1. 'OTHER-OBEYING'. Here the person is thinking in terms of some outside or *external authority* to which he feels deference – a god, a hero-figure, a sacred scripture, a priest. His emotions here might be basically fear of the authority, or admiration for it: a feeling of dependence on it, a desire to stand well with it, and so on.

2. 'SELF-OBEYING'. Here the person obeys something *within himself* – his 'conscience', his feelings of guilt or shame, his ideal of himself, his own compulsions and impulses. These feelings are taken as valid in their own right. Such a person might say, for instance: I just couldn't live with myself if I was a thief: I'm a good Christian (Buddhist, etc.) and good Christians don't steal – I'd be too ashamed, and so on.

3. 'SELF-CONSIDERING'. Here the person considers his own advantage. A Christian who believes that he ought not to steal because he will go to hell if he does, or that he ought to die a martyr's

death in the arena because he will gain a great reward in heaven,
is thinking in this way. The emotions here are straightforward
desires for advantage, and fear of disadvantage or un-
pleasantness.

4. 'OTHER-CONSIDERING'. Here the person's feelings include an important element of love or concern for other people. If
I think it wrong to steal because it is not nice for other people –
and never mind what any authority says, or what my 'conscience'
tells me, or what is to my own advantage – then I am thinking in
this mode.

Now as I have tried to show in another book[1] these 'modes of
thought' appear to a greater or lesser extent in most religions and
other outlooks. What I want to consider here is the way in which
they intermingle and succeed each other *in the same religion* and
in the same religious believer. This is, in fact, not very surprising;
for the emotions that go with the 'modes' are common to all men.
But it needs to be brought out, if only to see how complicated a
business it is to determine exactly what feelings are going on 'under
the surface'.

Two 'mixed' examples
We can begin with two simple cases where the same person is using
more than one 'mode'. Notice here how quickly the different
modes – and this means, the different emotions – follow and inter-
lock with each other:

Example 1
Our first example comes from Homer's *Iliad*.[2] In the following
passage, Hector is explaining to his wife why he thinks he ought to
go out from Troy and fight with the Greeks, rather than staying
safely in the city as his wife has asked him to do:

> I am indeed concerned about all the things you have said, wife. But
> I should be terribly ashamed of myself in front of the Trojans and
> the long-robed Trojan women, if like a coward I were to stand
> aside and shirk the fighting. Nor does my own heart tell me to do
> so, since I have learned to behave nobly, and always to fight

[1] *Ideals* (Lutterworth Press).
[2] Book VI, 440ff.

amongst the Trojan leaders, so as to gain great honour for my father and myself. For I know well enough in my mind and my heart that the day will come when holy Troy will perish. . . .

The logic of this is: (1) I am not unmoved by considerations of my own safety (SELF-CONSIDERING) or the safety of my wife and child (OTHER-CONSIDERING). But (2) what would the Trojans think of me if I didn't fight? (OTHER-OBEYING). In any case (3) I wouldn't feel right in myself – I have been brought up to be a noble champion (SELF-OBEYING). So I shall fight, though not because (4) I think it is likely to help Troy in the long run (OTHER-CONSIDERING), for I know well enough that Troy will fall.

Hector is here mostly influenced by the OTHER-OBEYING and SELF-OBEYING modes, not by the other two. As very often with ideals concerned with 'honour', 'nobility', etc. it is difficult to separate the OTHER-OBEYING from the SELF-OBEYING. In (2), he talks about the feeling of shame he would have if he shirked the fight, but relates this particularly to the Trojans: it seems to be a matter of what they would think of him rather than what he would think of himself. He distinguishes this from (3), his own inner feelings ('Nor' – a further point – 'does my own heart tell me . . .'). But they are closely related. In any case, we can at least distinguish these from the two CONSIDERING modes, which he explicitly rejects in (1) and (4). He is not moved by questions like 'What's the *use* of it?', 'Whom does it *help*?', etc. but by an ideal of honour.

Example 2
The next example is from Jesus' words as reported in St Luke's Gospel:

And as ye would that men should do to you, do ye also to them likewise. For if ye love them which love you, what thank have ye? for sinners also love those that love them. And if ye do good to them which do good to you, what thank have ye? for sinners also do even the same . . . But love ye your enemies, and do good, and lend, hoping for nothing again; and your reward shall be great, and ye shall be the children of the Highest: for he is kind unto the unthankful and to the evil. Be ye therefore merciful, as your Father also is merciful.

The logic of this is: Do as you would be done by, because (1) if you don't you're no better than ordinary sinners are (SELF-OBEY-ING: cf. 'Big boys don't do that sort of thing', 'You don't want to behave like a baby, do you?', etc.): (2) you will be well rewarded for it (SELF-CONSIDERING): (3) you will be more like God (SELF-OBEYING, living up to an internalized ideal).

'Historical' examples

If the 'modes' and emotions are many and various in one individual at one time, it is clear that they may vary even more if we consider the history of particular religions and outlooks. How it is that, as history proceeds, the tone and quality of these outlooks change so radically? We must not forget that the alterations are, so to speak, a *reshuffling* of the emotions already in the hearts of the believers: certain emotions or modes become dominant at certain times, and then give way to others. How and why does this happen?

1. A general account

It happens, of course, for all sorts of reasons; and shortly we shall give some examples. But it is possible to give a general account of some of the most important factors.

(a) First, many ideals were associated with particular 'founders' or 'originators'. These originators were private individuals who did not, for the most part, hold any great responsibility in public life. This is true, for instance of Jesus, Buddha, Lao-Tse, Epicurus, Marx, Freud, Sartre and many others. Of course there are also public men who put forward what were certainly in some sense 'ideals' – Pericles, Hitler and Lenin, for instance – but these were not usually universal ideals intended for all humanity: they were for the most part ideals referring to a particular nation, or a particular historical period.

(b) Secondly, such men were often what is called 'charismatic' figures: that is, men of outstanding personal qualities, with sufficient magnetic force to impress themselves (and their ideals) firmly on their fellow-men. This was partly because many of them practised what they preached. As a result of this, many of them acquired small groups of friends, associates or disciples who were devoted to them personally, and practised their ideals.

(c) Thirdly, the ideals they put forward, although often different, tended to make severe demands on ordinary people. (This is indeed hardly surprising, since if it were not the case they would not be known as 'great' moralists or thinkers.) In almost all cases, their ideals were more high-minded or sophisticated than most ordinary people of their time could easily attain to.

It is not hard to see how these three factors, individually and collectively, produce a state of affairs which is unlikely to last long, and which is therefore likely to change for better or worse:

(a) First, if the ideal meets with any public success, it will become (to use a jargon term) *institutionalized*: that is, it will be incorporated into some form of organization (a church, a political party, etc.). But such institutions and organizations are not often able to devote themselves entirely to keeping alive the original spirit of the ideal: they have to deal more with the practical world, with politics and war and social changes of various kinds. Hence in the rough-and-tumble of everyday living the original ideal is likely to be changed, just because it is incorporated in an institutional form. The leaders of the organization will now not be private individuals, as were the original inventors of the ideal, but public men with a public job to do: archbishops, politicians, party leaders, and so forth. Consciously or unconsciously, they will change the spirit of the original ideal to suit worldly circumstances.

(b) Secondly, the original 'charismatic' founders, and the devoted groups which were attached to them, do not live for ever. By memory, ritual or scripture their second-generation followers may try, as it were, to keep them alive: but in fact they die, and their immediate influence wanes. Hence it is natural that in the course of time the original spirit of the ideal becomes *diluted*, or misunderstood, or deliberately altered, as subsequent generations replace the founding fathers. Further, if the ideal is successful it becomes more widely shared – it extends throughout space, over

greater numbers of people, as well as through time: and in this
process also it is likely to change and lose something of its original
force. For that force depended partly on the operation of the ideal
in a small and devoted group: when it is scattered throughout the
world, it is not surprising that changes occur.

(c) Thirdly, the demands made by the ideal are unlikely to be met,
because they are too severe for most people. Hence it is likely that
people will 'interpret' – or in effect *change* – the ideal so as to suit
themselves. People need ideals, and like to think of themselves as
'good so-and-sos' (good Christians, Communists, Buddhists, etc.):
and if they are to be able to do this, the ideals have to be recast into
a more manageable and easier form. One common way of doing
this is to forget about the original *spirit* of the ideal, and follow
only the 'letter of the law' – the prescribed rituals, the easy and
obvious outward signs of being a 'good so-and-so' – so that they
can still pretend that they are following the ideal itself. But in fact
they have altered it.

It is important to notice that the change may be for better *or*
worse. I have perhaps made it sound, by the use of such words as
'dilution', 'easier', 'suit themselves', and so on in the above para-
graphs, as if all or most of such changes were for the worse; but
this is not necessarily so. Thus, to take (a) above, it may be that an
ideal loses by being institutionalized: that, in the rough-and-
tumble of everyday life, the original spirit of (say) Socialism or
Communism or Christianity becomes degraded: it turns, perhaps,
into mere party politics or cynicism, the leaders of the institution
become interested only in their own power and prestige, and so
forth. But it may also turn out the other way: it may be that the
original ideal was somewhat wild, extremist, utopian or in other
ways unreasonable, and that by having to meet the test of the
everyday world, of 'practical politics', it becomes changed or re-
interpreted into a more satisfactory and sensible form.

This might be true, in the same sort of way, as regards (b) and
(c) above. In (b), the original 'charismatic' leader and his group
vanish; they may be replaced by a half-hearted, week-kneed set of
followers: but they may be replaced by followers who are more
sensible, less doctrinaire and in general saner than the original

founders. Similarly, in (c), although recasting the original ideal so as to make it easier for most people may result in its degeneration, this may also result in making it more useful, more practicable, and less airy-fairy than it was before. Everything thus depends on the particular case: on the merits and demerits of the original ideal, and on what happens to it in its subsequent history. We cannot prejudge the issue: we can only look at the facts.

We must remember that hitherto we have been concerned with classifying ideals in terms of logical modes of thought: so that if a set of people use one mode of thought, and then this set (or another set calling themselves by the same name) start using another quite different mode, we shall say – in this context – that the ideal has been replaced by another. In these terms words like 'Christianity', 'Communism', etc. may stand for many different ideals, since people who called themselves Christians, Communists, etc. have used many different modes of thought. But what we are now doing is different. We are now talking of ideals and outlooks in a more historical way, and trying to see how outlooks which may continue to be called 'Christian', 'Communist', etc. become changed in the course of time.

Example 1

Our first example comes from classical Greek history. In 431 B.C., Athens was at war with Sparta. Pericles, a man of powerful personality and with a devoted group of friends and supporters, was the most influential person in Athens; and in a speech made to the Athenians he sets out an ideal for the Athenians to follow, which many of them would at that time have agreed with. What he says is this:

> Just as our political life is free and open, so is our day-to-day life in our relations with each other. We do not get into a state with our next-door neighbour if he enjoys himself in his own way, nor do we give him the kind of black looks which, though they do no real harm, still do hurt people's feelings. We are free and tolerant in our private lives; but in public affairs we keep to the law. This is because it commands our deep respect.
> Again, in questions of general good feeling there is a great contrast between us and most other people. We make friends by doing

good to others, not by receiving good from them. This makes our friendship all the more reliable, since we want to keep alive the gratitude of those who are in our debt by showing continued good-will to them: whereas the feelings of one who owes us something lack the same enthusiasm, since he knows that, when he repays our kindness, it will be more like paying back a debt than giving some-thing spontaneously. We are unique in this. When we do kind-nesses to others, we do not do them out of any calculations of profit or loss: we do them without afterthought, relying on our free liber-ality. Taking everything together then, I declare that our city is an education to Greece, and I declare that in my opinion each single one of our citizens, in all the manifold aspects of life, is able to show himself the rightful lord and owner of his own person, and do this, moreover, with exceptional grace and exceptional versatility. And to show that this is no empty boasting for the present occasion, but real tangible fact, you have only to consider the power which our city possesses and which has been won by those very qualities which I have mentioned.[1]

Now this speech was made early in the war, at a time when Athens was doing well. Athenian power rested on an empire, whose subject states paid money to Athens: the Athenians used this money to maintain their fleet and army. It was thus important to Athens that the money should continue to flow in. In Pericles' time, there was comparatively little difficulty; but as the war went on, more and more of the subject states in the empire began to rebel and refused to pay; and Pericles, who died shortly after making the speech quoted above, was replaced by other politicians of a less altruistic and benevolent kind, who organized the col-lection of the money along more professional and tougher lines. Hence Athens began to look around for small states who could be incorporated into the empire and made to pay up, without worry-ing too much about whether this was right or just.

We can see here, then, how our three factors operated. (a) First, the altruistic and benevolent ideal which Pericles put forward – an ideal of how to behave towards other people – had to stand up to the actual political institutions and situations of the time: the existence of the empire, the collection of the money, the military weakness of Athens, the politicians' need to keep the empire going

[1] Translation of Thucydides, here and below, by Rex Warner (Penguin Classics).

in order to secure their own power. (b) With the death of Pericles, and the dispersal of his closest supporters, his ideal became diluted and distorted. (c) It became too hard for the average Athenian, particularly under the increasingly tough conditions of war-time, to give his support to such an unselfish ideal. In consequence we should not be too surprised that, within only fifteen years, the Athenians are playing a very different tune.

In 416 B.C., the Athenians decided to conquer the small island of Melos. They had no justification at all for this: the Melians were harmless, wished to be neutral, and had no sort of treaty or alliance with Athens. Part of the dialogue between the Athenians and the Melians goes like this:

> *Melians:* No one can object to each of us putting forward our own views in a calm atmosphere. That is perfectly reasonable. What is scarcely consistent with such a proposal is the present threat – indeed the certainty – of your making war on us. We see that you have come prepared to judge the argument your-selves; and that the likely end of it all will be either war, if we prove that we are in the right, and so refuse to surrender – or else slavery.

> *Athenians:* Then we on our side will use no fine phrases saying, for example, that we have a right to our empire because we defeated the Persians, or that we have come against you now because of the injuries you have done us – a great mass of words that nobody would believe. And we ask you on your side not to imagine that you will influence us by saying that you, though a colony of Sparta, have not joined Sparta in the war, or that you have never done us any harm. Instead we recommend that you should try to get what it is possible for you to get, taking into consideration what we both really do think; since you know as well as we do that, when these matters are discussed by practical people, the standard of jus-tice depends on the equality of power to compel and that in fact the strong do what they have the power to do and the weak what they have to accept.

> *Melians:* Then in our view (since you force us to leave justice out of account and to confine ourselves to self-interest) – in our view it is at any rate useful that you should not destroy a principle that is to the general good of all men – namely, that in the case of all who fall into danger there should be such a

thing as fair play and just dealing, and that such people should be allowed to use and to profit by arguments that fall short of a mathematical accuracy. And this is a principle which affects you as much as anybody, since your own fall would be visited by the most terrible vengeance and would be an example to the world.

Athenians: As for us, even assuming that our empire does come to an end, we are not despondent about what would happen next. One is not so much frightened of being conquered by a power which rules over others, as Sparta does (not that we are concerned with Sparta now), as of what would happen if a ruling power is attacked and defeated by its own subjects. So far as this point is concerned, you can leave it to us to face the risks involved. What we shall do is to show you that it is for the good of our own empire that we are here and that it is for the preservation of your city that we shall say what we are going to say. We do not want trouble in bringing you into our empire, and we want you to be spared for the good both of yourselves and of ourselves.

Melians: And how could it be just as good for us to be the slaves as for you to be the masters?

Athenians: You, by giving in, would save yourselves from disaster; we, by not destroying you, would be able to profit from you.

Melians: So you would not agree to our being neutral, friends instead of enemies, but allies of neither side?

Athenians: No, because it is not so much your hostility that injures us; it is rather the case that, if we were on friendly terms with you, our subjects would regard that as a sign of weakness in us, whereas your hatred is evidence of our power.

Melians: Is that your subjects' idea of fair play – that no distinction should be made between people who are quite unconnected with you and people who are mostly your own colonists or else rebels whom you have conquered?

Athenians: So far as right and wrong are concerned they think that there is no difference between the two, that those who still preserve their independence do so because they are strong, and that if we fail to attack them it is because we are afraid. So that by conquering you we shall increase not only the size but the security of our empire. We rule the sea and you are islanders, and weaker islanders too than the others; it is therefore particularly important that you should not escape.

Eventually, the Athenians captured Melos, and behaved with the utmost cruelty. In Thucydides' words, they 'put to death all the men of military age whom they took, and sold the women and children as slaves'. Compare this with Pericles' remark above: 'We make friends by doing good to others, not by receiving good from them'. What has happened here is, quite simply, that the ideal has changed from the 'other-considering' mode to the 'self-considering' mode.

Example 2

Our second example is an example of an improvement rather than a distortion. It comes from the history of Jewish thought, as illustrated in the Old Testament and elsewhere. At one stage of their history, the Jews (or at least their law-makers) seem to have thought primarily in the 'self-obeying' and 'other-obeying' modes, and to have subscribed to a large number of very severe rules and regulations, the breach of which was supposed to entail dire punishment. Nor is it clear that many of these rules and regulations had any point:

> Whatsoever parteth the hoof, and is clovenfooted and cheweth the cud, among the beasts, that shall ye eat. Nevertheless, these shall ye not eat . . . the rabbit, because he cheweth the cud but divideth not the hoof; he is unclean unto you. And the hare . . . and the swine . . . and the little owl and the cormorant and the great owl and the swan and the pelican . . . Ye shall eat the blood of no manner of flesh; for the life of all flesh is the blood thereof: whosoever eateth it shall be cut off . . . thou shalt not have sexual intercourse with mankind as with womankind: it is abomination . . . they shall surely be put to death . . . If a girl that is a virgin is married unto a husband, and a man find her in the city and sleep with her, then shall ye bring them both out and ye shall stone them with stones that they die . . . and if a man cause a harm to his neighbour, as he hath done so shall it be done to him: harm for harm, eye for eye, tooth for tooth . . . And Moses spake to the children of Israel that they should bring forth him that had cursed and stone him with

stones. And the children of Israel did as the Lord commanded Moses.[1]

This represents an early stage in Jewish history, in which the outlook we are considering could hardly be described as an 'ideal' at all. It is, rather, a set of rigid taboos, ritual prohibitions and primitive rules; reminding us of the kind of thinking which is sometimes found in very young children, who have something of the same simple-minded sense of retributive justice and taboos. These rules, backed by God (Jehovah), simply had to be obeyed: they were *the* rules, and were not supposed to be questioned.

As time went on, however, there was a significant change. One might say that the Jews began to *grow up*. Whilst still retaining the general framework of 'what God commands' and 'the law that Moses brought from God', they began to interpret or fill in this framework differently. We may again point to our three factors of change: (a) The political circumstances of the Jews changed: in particular they had more contact with alien peoples, so that the very tough and tribalistic system of taboos began to seem less important for daily living: (b) Moses himself died, and became an almost legendary figure to whom new interpretations of the law could be attached: (c) the severity of the law began to seem too hard, or too unnecessary, for the majority of ordinary people. But whatever the causes, later Jewish writers are obviously concerned to *look behind* the law for what they took to be the really important things. And these things are much more in the 'other-considering' mode (though still within the framework of 'what God commands' or 'what the law means').

This later ideal of the good man, the man 'acceptable to God', is given by the writer of the Psalms in these words:

He that walketh uprightly, and worketh righteousness, and speaketh the truth in his heart. He that backbiteth not with his tongue, nor doeth evil to his neighbour ... He that promiseth to his neighbour and disappointeth him not.

By Isaiah:

He that walketh righteously and speaketh uprightly; he that des-

[1] Extracts from *Leviticus*.

piseth gain derived from oppression, and that keepeth his hand from bribes.

And by Micah:

> What doth the Lord require of thee but to do justly, and to love mercy ... ?

This is already a very different sort of outlook: and the change becomes virtually complete with the later Rabbis and the coming of Jesus. Whilst Jesus too used the framework of 'the law' and 'what is pleasing to God', it is plain from the following quotations how much the spirit or content of the Jewish ideal has been changed:

> If thou bring thy gift to the altar and there rememberest that thy brother has something against thee, leave there thy gift before the altar and go thy way: first be reconciled to thy brother, and then come and offer thy gift ... Ye have heard that it hath been said 'An eye for an eye, and a tooth for a tooth'. But I say unto you, that ye resist not evil: but whosoever shall smite thee on thy right cheek, turn to him the other also ... Give to him that asketh thee, and from him that would borrow from thee turn not away. Ye have heard that it hath been said 'Thou shalt love thy neighbour and hate thine enemy'. But I say unto you, love your enemies, bless them that curse you, do good to them that hate you, pray for them which despitefully use you and persecute you ... For if ye forgive men their trespasses, your heavenly Father will also forgive you: but if ye forgive not men their trespasses, neither will your Father forgive your trespasses ... Judge not, that ye be not judged ... And why beholdest thou the mote that is in thy brother's eye and considerest not the beam that is in thine own eye?[1]

Example 3

Our final example is longer and comes from the history of Christianity. The original Christian ideal passed through a great many different stages. Some of these certainly seem to be distortions of the original ideal: others stress certain aspects of it, or add to it in various ways: others again may be seen as an attempt to recapture its original spirit. As is to be expected in the case of an ideal which

---

[1] Extracts from the Gospels.

has prevailed for nearly 2,000 years, its history is long and complicated: and it is difficult to speak of 'the Christian ideal' in any very clear sense. For the Christian church divided into various sects (Roman Catholic and Greek Orthodox, Protestants, Lutherans, Baptists, Wesleyans, Quakers, etc.) that supported ideals which were significantly different: and the ideals held by ordinary Christians may well have been different from those promulgated by the leaders of the church. Hence we cannot of course here do anything like justice to even part of the actual history of 'the Christian ideal': we shall simply try to illustrate one aspect of it, by two or three brief sketches.

(a) It is plausible to regard a great part of the 'original Christian ideal' as essentially concerned with love, brotherly affection, kindness, human equality, and similar principles in the 'other-considering' mode of thought. This is not of course to deny the 'other-obeying' belief in God and Christ on the part of the early Christians: but the *kind* of God they worshipped is to some extent revealed in their moral attitude. The early Christian communities are said to have 'had all things in common', and their members regarded each other as brothers and sisters. Even an external non-Christian observer, investigating them for the Roman emperor, seems to have believed that they did nothing worse than 'meet before dawn on a fixed day, sing an antiphonal hymn to Christ as God, and swear not to take part in any crime – not to steal, rob, commit adultery, cheat, or refuse to return money they had been entrusted with: and having done this, their custom was to go away, and come back to take a meal in common'. The letters of St Paul are full of such remarks as 'Love is the fulfilling of the law', 'If thine enemy hunger, feed him: if he thirst, give him drink', 'Husbands, love your wives', 'Recompense to no man evil for evil', 'Rejoice with them that rejoice, and weep with them that weep'. There is much more evidence of the same kind.

About three hundred years later, when Christianity was the official religion of the Roman Empire, we still find what seems to be the 'other-considering' mode at work. A historian[1] writes:

[1] W. E. H. Lecky, *History of European Morals*, (Longmans, 1902), Vol. II, pp. 79 and following.

Christianity for the first time made charity a rudimentary virtue, giving it a leading place in the moral type, and in the exhortations of its teachers. Besides its general influence in stimulating the affections, it effected a complete revolution in this sphere, by regarding the poor as the special representatives of the Christian Founder ... Even in the days of persecution, collections for the relief of the poor were made at the Sunday meetings. The agapae or feasts of love were intended mainly for the poor, and food that was saved by the fasts was devoted to their benefit. A vast organization of charity, presided over by the bishops, and actively directed by the deacons, soon ramified over Christendom, till the bond of charity became the bond of unity, and the most distant sections of the Christian Church corresponded by the interchange of mercy.

Even the early Oriental monks, who for the most part were extremely removed from the active and social virtues, supplied many noble examples of charity. St. Ephrem, in a time of pestilence, emerged from his solitude to found and superintend a hospital at Edessa. A monk named Thalasius collected blind beggars in an asylum on the banks of the Euphrates. A merchant named Apollonius founded on Mount Nitria a gratuitous dispensary for the monks. The monks often assisted by their labours provinces that were suffering from pestilence or famine. We may trace the remains of the pure socialism that marked the first phase of the Christian community, in the emphatic language with which some of the Fathers proclaimed charity to be a matter not of mercy but of justice, maintaining that all property is based on usurpation, that the earth by right is common to all men, and that no man can claim a superabundant supply of its goods except as an administrator for others. A Christian, it was maintained, should devote at least one-tenth of his profits to the poor.

(b) Yet, *at the same time*, we see one very remarkable and extreme distortion of the ideal: the ascetic movement, which reached its height some 250–300 years after Christ. Our historian points the contrast between this harsh, puritanical ideal and Christ's conduct – the teacher who began his mission at a marriage feast; who was continually reproached by his enemies for the readiness with which he mixed with the world, and who selected from the female sex some of his purest and most devoted followers.[1] For the

[1] Lecky, p. 105.

ascetic ideal was opposed to the 'world and the flesh', to anything physically pleasurable. Thus St James became a kind of ideal saint, a faithful picture of what, according to the notions of theologians, was the true type of human nobility. He 'was consecrated', it was said, 'from his mother's womb. He drank neither wine nor fermented liquors, and abstained from animal food. A razor never came upon his head. He never anointed himself with oil, or used a bath. He alone was allowed to enter the sanctuary. He never wore woollen, but linen, garments. He was in the habit of entering the temple alone, and was often found upon his bended knees, and interceding for the forgiveness of the people, so that his knees became as hard as a camel's'.[1]

This new ideal could be ascribed to several modes of thinking. Some of those who practised it claimed that God had commanded them to behave in this way ('other-obeying'): some that they would gain the rewards of heaven by it ('self-considering'). But there seems also to be a strong element of the 'self-obeying' mode: that is, certain interior feelings – particularly guilt about the body and the physical part of life – compelled them to adopt this curious ideal. Perhaps the most extreme example is St Simeon, of whom our author[2] writes:

> For a whole year, we are told, St Simeon stood upon one leg, the other being covered with hideous ulcers, while his biographer was commissioned to stand by his side, to pick up the worms that fell from his body, and to replace them in the sores, the saint saying to the worm, 'Eat what God has given you'. From every quarter pilgrims of every degree thronged to do him homage. A crowd of prelates followed him to the grave. A brilliant star is said to have shone miraculously over his pillar; the general voice of mankind pronounced him to be the highest model of a Christian saint.

This rampage of guilt and self-torture went hand in hand with another distortion of the ideal: the picture of eternal punishment in hell, as ordained by God ('other-obeying').

Although two or three amiable theologians had made faint and

---

[1] Lecky, quoting Eusebius, p. 105.

[2] Lecky, p. 112 (quoting Simeon's disciple Antony in the *Vita Patrum*, Evagrius, i. 13, 14).

altogether abortive attempts to question the eternity of pun-ishment; although there had been some slight difference of opinion concerning the future of some Pagan philosophers who had lived before the introduction of Christianity, and also upon the question whether infants who died unbaptized were only de-prived of all joy, or were actually subjected to never-ending agony, there was no question as to the main features of the Catholic doc-trine. According to the patristic theologians, it was part of the gospel revelation that the misery and suffering the human race endures upon earth is but a feeble image of that which awaits it in the future world; that all its members beyond the Church, as well as a very large proportion of those who are within its pale, are doomed to an eternity of agony in a literal and undying fire.

It is impossible to conceive more ghastly, grotesque, and material conceptions of the future world than they evince, or more hideous calumnies against that Being who was supposed to inflict upon His creatures such unspeakable misery. The devil was represented bound by red-hot chains, on a burning gridiron in the centre of hell. The screams of his never-ending agony made its rafters to resound; but his hands were free, and with these he seized the lost souls, crushed them like grapes against his teeth, and then drew them by his breath down the fiery cavern of his throat. Daemons with hooks of red-hot iron plunged souls alternately into fire and ice. Some of the lost were hung up by their tongues, others were sawn asunder, other gnawed by serpents, others beaten together on an anvil and welded into a single mass, others boiled and then strained through a cloth, others twined in the embraces of daemons whose limbs were of flame. The fire of earth, it was said, was but a picture of that of hell. The latter was so immeasurably more intense that it alone could be called real.[1]

(c) I have quoted these as the most extreme examples of the op-posite of what we should normally mean by 'love'. But of course there are many other possibilities. There is, for instance, the 'other-obeying' legalism of the Pharisees as portrayed in the New Testament, similar to that of the ancient Jews in our previous example[2]. There is the 'self-obeying' attachment to 'conscience' or intuitions of guilt. Both these played an important role in the later history of Christianity, particularly in the Reformation. But

[1] Lecky, p. 219–20.
[2] Example 2, pp. 81

in order to make the point most clearly, we shall omit all the twists
and turns of that history, and take a big jump in the 20th century.
Here it seems that some writers are trying to get back to the
original 'other-considering' ideal of Christianity. Consider John
Robinson.[1]

'It is love which is the constitutive principle – and law, at most, is
only the regulative one, if it is even that.'[2]

The classic illustration of this insistence in the teaching of Jesus,
that the sabbath is made for man and not man for the sabbath,
that compassion for *persons* overrides all law, is his shocking ap-
probation of David's action in placing human need (even his own)
above all regulations however sacrosanct:

'Have you not read what David did, when he was hungry, and
those who were with him: how he entered the house of God and
ate the bread of the Presence, which it was not lawful for him to
eat nor for those who were with him, but only for the priests?'[3]

It is, of course, a highly dangerous ethic and the representatives
of supranaturalistic legalism will, like the Pharisees,[4] always fear
it. Yet, I believe it is the only ethic for 'man come of age'. To resist
it in the name of religious sanctions will not stop it: it will only
ensure that the form it takes will be anti-Christian.

. . . For nothing can of itself always be labelled as 'wrong'. One
cannot, for instance, start from the position 'sex relations before
marriage' or 'divorce' are wrong or sinful in themselves. They may
be in 99 cases or even 100 cases out of 100, but they are not intrin-
sically so, for the only intrinsic evil is lack of love. Continence and
indissolubility may be the guiding norms of love's response; they
may, and should, be hedged about by the laws and conventions of
society, for these are the dykes of love in a wayward and loveless
world. But, morally speaking, they must be defended, as Fletcher
puts it, 'situationally, not prescriptively' – in other words, in terms
of the fact that persons matter, and the deepest welfare of these
particular persons in this particular situation matters, more than

[1] *Honest to God* (S.C.M. Press) p. 116 and following.
[2] Quoted from J. Fletcher, *Harvard Divinity Bulletin*, The New Look in Christian
Ethics, Oct. 1959.
[3] *Matt.* 12.3f., See the whole context *Matt.* 12.1–14.
[4] *Matt.* 12.14.

anything else in the world. Love's casuistry must cut deeper and must be more searching, more demanding, than anything required by the law, precisely because it goes to the heart of the individual personal situation. But we are bound in the end to say with Professor Fletcher: 'If the emotional and spiritual welfare of both parents and children in a *particular* family can be served best by a divorce, wrong and cheapjack as divorce commonly is, then love requires it'.[1]

It follows from this that to talk in a very general way of 'the Christian ideal', or to consider whether 'the Christian ideal' is right or wrong, good or bad, reasonable or unreasonable, is not very profitable. Nor is this example of Christianity the only one: indeed, we would have to search quite hard to find any examples of ideals or 'isms' which had not undergone very considerable changes of this kind. This is interesting from a historical point of view, but it is only helpful to the person who is trying to choose between various ideals if he realizes that it is the four modes of thought which are fundamental, and not the titles of the various 'isms'. The real choice is not whether to be 'a Christian', 'a humanist', 'an existentialist', 'a Communist', etc.: for all these titles are too vague, and cover too much ground, to be of any use to us. How can we say 'Yes' or 'No' to the question 'Were the ideals of ancient Athens admirable?', now that we have seen (Example 1) how these ideals changed within only twenty years? Or to the question 'Was the morality of the Jews, as described in the Old Testament, a good one?', now that we can see the difference between Moses and Isaiah (Example 2)? Or to the question 'Should one behave like a Christian?', now that we have seen (Example 3) that Christians are apt to think and act in diametrically opposite ways?

[1] *Honest to God*.

G

ten

'Making Sense' and 'Ultimate Questions'

In this chapter I want to return to a phenomenon briefly mentioned in Part I. It is a phenomenon which is peculiar to our own times (though not entirely confined to them), and there is a great deal of talk and writing about it. I refer to the use of religion as a way of 'making sense' of life, or of giving us an answer to 'ultimate questions'.

For many people today, particularly in highly-developed industrialized societies, formal religion has lost much of its force. Fewer of us than before find a complete 'answer to life' in terms of a particular Christian sect: and the same applies, perhaps to a lesser extent, to other countries in which other religions are current (though some, like Russia and China, have abandoned religion altogether, at least officially). But, though formal religion does not give us an acceptable 'answer', we still want to ask the questions – questions like 'Who am I?', 'What is it all for?', 'What is the purpose of life?', 'Why am I here?', and so on. A good deal – perhaps the greater part – of modern talk 'about religion' seems to be concerned with such questions; and though we may not think that such talk is strictly about *religion* (only about 'attitudes to life'), nevertheless it is important. What sort of attitude should we have to it?

First, philosophers have shown that these questions are *odd* or *problematic*. That does not make them disreputable; but it should make us think about the questions before trying to answer them. 'What is everything for?' is obviously not like 'What is a hammer for?'; 'What is the meaning of life,' is not like 'What is the meaning of this code?'; 'Who am I?' and 'Why am I here?' are not to be answered by, e.g., 'Your name is Jane Smith and you're here to attend an interview for . . .' We suggested earlier that many such 'questions' are often more like laments, or expressions of anxiety or doubt: those who ask them need reassurance, or psychological guidance, rather than 'answers' in a strict sense. The 'questions' are serious, but perhaps not serious as *questions*. Sometimes we know this quite well: if waking up on a black Monday morning with a grim week's work ahead I say 'Oh my God, what's it all for?' I know I am just groaning or feeling suicidal. But sometimes we deceive ourselves into supposing them to be ordinary questions with ordinary (if rather grand) answers.

Many people who encourage us to ask 'ultimate questions' do not regard them as problematic in this way. They may regard them as *difficult*, but that is not at all the same thing. 'What is the purpose of a fremkin-twisting swizzle-bolt?' is a difficult question, like 'Who is the twenty-seventh person in line of succession to the throne of England'; but 'What is the purpose of life?' and 'Who am I?' are not difficult in that way – they are, rather, mysterious questions whose *sense* is not clear. To treat them as if they had a clear sense and function is to display either ignorance or dishonesty. The natural and correct reaction of anyone who is not already addicted, by temperament or habit, to asking such questions would be 'I don't understand what the questions mean. What is the point of uttering these words? Ought one to utter them? What job do they do?'

Secondly, it is clear that some at least of these questions beg prior questions. This in two important ways, which need to be distinguished:

(a) There is the danger of assuming 'one right answer'. Phrases like '*the* purpose' of life, '*the* nature of man', '*the* meaning' of the universe, etc. illustrate this danger. Again, somebody who did not naturally think in this way would react by saying '*The* purpose? I don't know what you mean. I have lots of purposes in my life – I want to be happily married, get enough to eat, enjoy great works of art, and so on: what is this talk about "*the* purpose"?' The point reappears in statements beginning 'Life is . . .' (a glorious enterprise, doomed to ultimate tragedy, one damn thing after another, very difficult, etc.) The prior question begged here, then, is that there is some *one* 'answer' to these 'ultimate questions'.

(b) There is the deeper danger of so framing the questions that only one *sort* of answer will count. Roughly described, the kind of answer which I have in mind is one which allots people a *given role* and a *dependent status*. It is hard to say exactly what linguistic forms of the questions correlate with this, for much depends on the general mood of the questioner and the general (often unconscious) intentions behind the question. But it is reasonably clear, for instance, that such phrases as 'the purpose behind the universe', 'the meaning of life', and 'the design of the world' seem to beg for answers of this sort: that is, there is to be a discovery or realization of someone or something – not ourselves – who does the meaning, designing or purposing. 'God' is a natural answer to such questions, just because the questions already contain the concept of something like God: the concept of something other than ourselves that has purposes and plans. Often this concept is very vague: this 'other' is seen in some way as the universe itself or its 'spirit', or a 'power' or even 'human nature'. Often it is more naïve, and framed in terms of 'the divine law', 'God's commandments', and so on. But the concept is already written into the questions; and of course the prior question is whether we should do this writing-in at all – and this means, in effect, whether we should ask such questions, or at least ask them in that (question-begging) form.

Thus one author[1] writes: 'Religious education is fundamentally concerned with the education of attitudes, not with the study of cultures, nor with the assessment of systems of belief (though, of course, both the latter play their part in the former). It is concerned with the pupil's development of a faith in which to travel through life'.

As with many other such statements, one is here in doubt about which way the author would jump on a number of crucial issues; in particular about how far he is interested in anything one could strictly call religion. Our problem is to know what would count as a child's having developed 'a faith', 'a sense of direction', 'a valid perspective', etc. The possibilities are:

[1] Colin Alves, *Times Educational Supplement*, 24th March, 1967.

(a) Some particular religious faith (thus Christianity might count, but Buddhism and Islam not);

(b) Any religious faith (Christianity and perhaps Buddhism would count, but Marxism not);

(c) The right sort of religious faith (Christianity, perhaps Buddhism, but not Baal-Worship);

(d) The right sort of faith, not necessarily religious (perhaps existentialism or humanism might count, but Marxism or materialism not);

(e) Any sort of overall creed or metaphysic;

(f) Simply the right sort of attitudes, a 'healthy' outlook on life, etc.

No doubt the author regards some of these as unreal choices: as a Christian he may think, for instance, that in practice the Christian faith (a) is the only one that will give a child the right perspective or a 'healthy' outlook (f). But the truth of this, and of any other such particular propositions, has to be shown. Conceptually (a)–(f) are all different; and if we are setting out a statement of aims, we have to decide between them. Only (f), in fact, is wholly unexceptionable to any rational person: for all the others assume the merits of a particular faith, or of a particular type of faith, or of the notion 'Having a (any) faith'. As we have seen earlier, this cannot be assumed.

The distinction between (e) and (f) – between anything that we could reasonably call a 'faith' and just a 'healthy outlook' – is very blurred: and the terms used by the author ('sense of direction', 'valid perspective') do nothing to sharpen it. It is commonplace in psychological writings that the mentally healthy person will not live purely for the moment, but will have a number of long term aims: that he will incorporate a number of different aspects of his life within these aims: that he will have a 'sense of proportion', approach life with confidence and happiness, and so forth. Psychologists with a preference for a metaphysical diction may express some of these truisms by saying that such a person's life will be 'meaningful', or that he will be 'sustained by his faith in life', or 'find value in human existence' (a phrase also used in the same article). If this is all that is meant by 'a faith to live by', then we can make no objection: for all that these phrases point to are criteria of rationality or 'mental health'. But if it is meant that the rational or 'mentally healthy' individual must assent to a number of propositions about 'the meaning', or 'the purpose', of life, and about the 'supernatural': and in particular if it is meant that he should regard himself as in some way *placed* in the world by some external super-being, Nature, Life-Force or whatever, whose purpose and intentions he is bound to accede to; then such a view seems highly dubious.

These difficulties emerge in another way. If we ask questions about 'the nature of man' then we can approach this from the viewpoint of various disciplines. The biology teacher can tell us about a man's body, the historian about his history, the psychologist . . . and so on. In order to do this sort of thing effectively, we have to ensure that we can distinguish clearly between the disciplines; this means that we have to distinguish between the different logical types of questions which the disciplines answer. Questions which demand one sort of evidence (scientific), we refer to scientists: questions demanding knowledge of past human behaviour, to the historians: questions about human motives to the psychologist. If – what rarely happens in practice – we are really clear about this, we cannot help but be baffled when we find ourselves (or some of us) wanting to go on from there to ask 'ultimate questions'. 'The scientists, historians, etc. have told us something of the "nature of man", but this doesn't feel enough for us. What is his *real* nature? What *is* the universe really – yes, we know all what the scientists say, but it's not sufficient. Can't the religious people tell us the "answer" to these "ultimate questions"?' But then we go on 'Yes, but what *sort* of questions are they? Under what discipline do they fall? What sort of evidence or verification counts here? Are they indeed really *questions*? In fact, what are we really talking *about*?'

It seems plain that many at least of such questions are, to say the least, closely connected with the questioner's moods and emotions. They bear witness to the questioner's desire not only (or even chiefly) for a *correct* outlook on life, but for an emotionally satisfying one – one which makes him feel secure, 'alive', worth-while, that gives 'meaning' or 'purpose' to his life, that 'makes sense' of the world for him. How exactly we re-phrase these 'questions' may not much matter: what matters is that we recognize and explore the connection with the emotions. This is the point which is of prime practical importance.

We do not need psychologists to tell us that everyone has to 'make sense' of life; but we can see, I think, that there are different ways of doing this. One way leads naturally to these 'ultimate questions' – to the *asking* of them, not just to answering them in a certain manner. We might describe this way as follows: Some people feel the urge to look at 'life' or 'the world' as a whole, to ask questions about it and to seek for some single 'answer', 'meaning', or 'purpose' in it or given to it by some 'other', not ourselves. They may 'find' a meaning or purpose and be happy, or fail to 'find' one and despair. But both these are essentially similar: more like each other than either is like another range of people who do not feel this urge, people (we might say) who are not by nature inclined to metaphysics or to 'holistic' (all-embracing) views of the world.

The kind of move made here, which some psychologists call 'projection', is familiar to us. These people talk as if their doubts, worries, and questions are *about the world*: does it have 'meaning' or is it 'empty'? Is there a purpose behind it all or not? Other people relate their doubts and questions more *to themselves*: why do *I* feel depressed? Is it right for *me* to pursue such-and-such a goal? This (very briefly and inadequately described) distinction seems to me of fundamental importance. It is one thing to say 'Life has no meaning/purpose': quite another to say '*My* life has no meaning/purpose'. In the former case I accuse, or consider, or question 'life' or the 'universe': in the latter I accuse or consider myself – my own attitudes, emotions, pictures of the world, and so on.

The same psychological work is done by both types of people. For both are concerned with their worries, anxieties, insecurities, etc. One copes with them by asking whether there is anything 'outside' his normal experience – a God, a 'meaning', a 'power' – which will (he thinks) diminish his insecurity; the other looks either at himself or at his normal experience, hoping to achieve the same end. The difference lies in the level of sophistication. For the 'answers' given by the former will be projections of what he misses in himself or his normal life – a father-God who will tell him what to do, a 'divine law' which will solve his moral problems for him, a 'power' which will give him magic strength, or whatever. He will people the world, or structure it in such a way as to make himself feel safe and 'alive'. The latter does not try to resolve his difficulties by projection, but in some other way: perhaps he tolerates more anxiety, or tries to find satisfaction in the normal experiences of life, or goes to a psychiatrist, or takes drugs, or whatever.

If I have criticized the asking and answering of 'ultimate questions', this is because my guess is that, in practice, many askers and answerers are engaging in projective fantasy in this way. There is other evidence for this besides the linguistic forms which I have mentioned. It is characteristic both of young children, and of the history of religions, that human beings act in this way; and the correlation between the kind of psychological problems they have and the kind of fantasy-beings with which they populate the world is evident as soon as we make any close study, either of young children or of mentally ill adults, or of specific religions. But this is not to say anything against religion *per se*; nor – more relevantly to our present concern – is it to say anything against the asking of very general questions about 'life', 'the world', etc. Everything turns on the spirit in which the questions are asked, the purpose of asking them, and the way in which possible 'answers' are considered.

Again, very roughly, the crucial distinction will be between those who are concerned with *correctness* or *appropriateness* and those who are merely anxious to create a picture which satisfies themselves (and into which, as projective fantasy-makers commonly do, they desire to draw other people). That some attitude, or attitudes, to life is desirable: that there are more or less appropriate (or sane, or correct) emotions in the face of certain realities: that there are questions about how one *ought* to picture the world and parts of the world: and that consideration of these matters may begin by the asking of very general questions about 'the meaning of life' – all these seem obvious truths. But, when it comes to the point, a man is either concerned with what is right, true or appropriate, or else merely interested in satisfying his own feelings; and the sign of good teaching or discussion of such matters will be that those involved are constantly anxious to stick to the former and put the latter aside. They will bear continuously in mind the notions of *truth*, *evidence* and *criteria*, and be concerned to shoot down any kind of wishful thinking, however subtle or high-minded.

If 'ultimate questions' are asked and answered in this spirit, well and good. But (to return to our point of departure) anyone who does so in this spirit will be bound to be worried by the mere asking of the questions themselves. There are questions about what is true, which are settled by reference to particular disciplines or fields of study: not all of these, of course, are included in the term 'scientific' – there are procedures for discovering truth in law, history, morality, and aesthetics – but all of them involve prior clarity about what is to count as evidence. There are also questions equally involving the notions of correctness or appropriateness – equally 'objective', if we must use this misleading term – about what our feelings and desires ought to be, both in general and under particular circumstances: questions about the rightness or wrongness of our inner attitudes and emotions. There are also laments, groans, fantasies, hopes, illusions, expressions of various emotions and other phenomena. We have to be able to distinguish these clearly, and help our friends to do so. 'Ultimate questions' seem to me a very dangerous basis, precisely because they seem unconsciously designed to blur these crucial distinctions: under cover of them, a man may easily forget about evidence, take a fantasy for a statement of truth, mistake an expression of feeling for a claim to correctness.

We may fear that without raising such questions we will remain sunk in a world which seems (to us at least) restricted, tied to the banal interests of money-making, pleasure-seeking, following fashion, and so on. But we have, first, to recognize that the very move of saying 'Yes, yes, life is certainly a matter of making money and enjoying oneself and X and Y and Z – but don't you feel there must be more to it, something "out there", some unperceived reality, some "true meaning"?' may itself be mistaken. Again, everything turns on the spirit in which this is said. If we are trying, for instance, to show a contented pig that Socratic inquiry is also worth-while to enlarge our horizons by adding Beethoven to pop music, to consider life in a more long-term way, to see why love is more important than television, etc. – then there is no problem: we know where we are, what we mean, and (in broad outline) how to develop these various types of awareness. But if this approach seems too part-and-parcel to us, if none of these 'realities' is sufficient, if we still want to ask 'But what is it all *for*, what's the real meaning of it all?' – then we should beware. For now we are confused, at least: and probably worse.

We will wonder whether we are not ourselves in the grip of fantasy in believing – if indeed we have ever faced the question squarely – that *this* method of 'enlarging our horizons' is the most effective. For it bears marks of projection. We feel that we and others are restricted, blind, unaware: so, rather than consider in a more realistic ('scientific') way why this is so and what can be done about it, we fly at once to a consideration of the 'meaning' (one might almost say, 'the secret') of life. This single bold 'leap of faith', this sudden perception of the inner, real world of meaning and purpose that is inherent in or lies behind the universe – this is what will, at a blow, shed over us the required light. We offer a single elixir or panacea – the understanding of 'the meaning of life'. What we do not do is to submit ourselves to the slow, difficult process of inducing awareness in respect of *different* parts of 'the world' or 'life'. We could look at the glories of art, the wonders of nature, the depth of our own psychology, the fascinating complexity of moral problems, and so on; and we know that initiating ourselves into these is a long, hard job. So we try a short cut: we seek for something 'beyond' all these, which will do the job for us.

In point of fact, as any psychologist will tell you, the kinds of factors which 'restrict horizons', 'inhibit awareness', etc. are likely to sound much more pedestrian. They include such things as security in childhood, the growth of linguistic competence, firm but loving parental discipline, and all the oft-repeated (if still little understood) phenomena to which researchers draw our attention. Only in the light of these phenomena can we begin to consider what practical methods may be most effective. Will experience of art awake awareness of new worlds, or is it more to do with human relationships? How far is discussion an appropriate technique, as against role-playing, mime, drama, films or group therapy? Do we need more Wordsworth or more Freud? These are stupid questions as they stand, because they suggest that methods are mutually exclusive: but, even when sensibly put (if we knew how) they are still hard to answer, simply because we have not done enough research to know. Meanwhile we have to guess: but our guesses can at least be well-informed and – more important – freed from our own fantasies (if we try hard enough).

eleven

Educating Ourselves in Religion

In this last chapter I want to sketch out the ways in which we can best pursue the subject of this book – that is, how we can educate ourselves in religion. We saw in Part I that religion was not *centrally* concerned with a number of other things with which it is commonly confused: religion is not primarily a matter of science, or history, or morals. It is about what we worship and what we ought to worship: what to do with characteristically religious emotions such as awe, reverence, guilt and so on. We have seen something of the connection between various actual religions and these human emotions in Part II.

Now there is no harm, and much good, in studying what we may call the 'fringe' aspects of religion – the history of the Christian church, the Bible as literature, the comparative beliefs and social backgrounds of Jews, Mohammedans, Buddhists, and so forth. In this way we can educate ourselves *about religions*. But it seems at least as important to educate ourselves *in religion*: that is, in reference to the emotions that – in ourselves as well as in other people – make up the 'stuff' of religious beliefs. How, in general, are we to do this?

Content

We must take care not to throw too much out of the window. As we have seen in considering certain religions, a great many facts are relevant to our 'religious education' if they are attached and related to its central concern with emotions. For example, the case for knowing about church history, learning the Psalms by heart, or increasing our understanding of Christian doctrine as represented in the creeds, is a very weak one if it is based on the view that we ought to know about these things 'because it is part of our common culture'. (The same argument would apply to learning astrology in Babylonia, or voodoo in Haiti.) Similarly comparative religion may be useful as a kind of sociology or anthropology, but could hardly be justified as specifically religious education. But if these things are relevant to a better understanding of religious and other emotions – to an understanding of what it is, or what it feels like to have a religion – and if they are learned in that light and with that aim, then it is plain that we shall hesitate before throwing them out of the window. Thus, to choose an instance at random, we might reasonably think it important to be able to entertain the kind of feelings represented in, and evoked by, the Psalms or the first chapter of Genesis (perhaps Haydn's *Creation* would be better?), if we are to have an emotional grasp of what one type of religion, at least, is actually like.

We will thus probably want to use much of the traditional material as subject-matter, or as affording examples of particular religions (in much the same way as the teacher of morality may wish to use particular moral codes or *mores* as illustration-material). But the selection of the material will depend on whether it fulfils this particular purpose. Probably the most important kinds of material here will not consist of 'hard' historical facts (the journeys of St Paul, the history of the rise of Islam, etc.) but of psychological illustrations (what it *felt like* to believe in Jehovah or Aphrodite – do we feel anything of the same kind nowadays? – and so forth). We are concerned here with making real to ourselves such considerations as what sort of objects (gods) various people, today and in past history, are or have been in awe of and worshipped; why they have done so; how we ourselves feel about various objects of emotion (parents, nature, artistic productions that evoke emotion, etc.); whether these beliefs are reasonable, and so on. Psychological illustrations from primitive and poly-theistic religions may be particularly important here, at least as important as the study of the 'higher' religions.

This leads to a widening of our task. For though we will be concerned with objects of emotion as found in religion, we will also need some methods of getting ourselves to admit to, and hence to be more able to understand and control, our own emotions (awe, fear, loneliness, admiration, guilt and so forth) in relation the objects to which they are already attached: for these will be the stuff out of which our outlook – whether eventually religious or not – will be made. The relevant type of education is in general more analogous to certain types of psychotherapy than to subject-learning.

For example, suppose we are teachers dealing with adolescent boys whose 'outlook' is some form of 'honour ethic'. They are concerned not to lose face with their peers, to prove themselves tough and daring, to fulfil the code of honour which the gang or the group subscribes to: rather like the Japanese samurai, or gunfighters in Western films. This concern, we may think, is partly caused by their position as adolescents: they do not really feel big, tough, potent and adult; they have internal doubts about their own powers and their own security, and are anxious to prove themselves that these doubts can be laid to rest. Now here we have, if not exactly a religion, at any rate an outlook that incorporates many of the emotions which some religions (such as Christianity) would wish to be reorganized or redirected. Those adolescents may be in awe of, and even worship, the biggest and toughest person in their environment – perhaps the gang-leader, or some hero in the world of films or TV. They may repent and feel guilt – but not about their daring robberies, only about not being daring enough. They have their rituals, their conventions, their code – but these are not concerned to celebrate a loving God or a forgiving Christ, only to bind them more tightly to the service of honour.

Plainly, the only way in which teachers can hope to introduce them effectively to other outlooks or religions would be to start by making them more conscious of the outlook that they already have. If they are really to 'get the feel' of any other outlook (the Christian, for instance), they must be able to let go of their own, if only temporarily. They must be secure enough to detach their emotions from the 'honour ethic', and at least consider what it would be like to attach them to other objects. Otherwise, although we may tell them about other outlooks, these outlooks will seem to them mere oddities, and not appear as real and viable alternatives.

The teacher has to begin by getting them to understand their existing outlook, and the (often unconscious) reasons behind it, so that their emotions are no longer compulsively directed in the way they are.

Of course this is only one example: it is not only adolescent boys whose outlook is compulsive, and who hence find it virtually impossible to make any really free choice of outlook. But it suggests strongly that all of us should think hard about the conditions and the context in which this sort of education can flourish. Obviously a relationship of trust and closeness, in which we are prepared to take even the first steps in trying to understand ourselves, is essential. As soon as one even starts to think seriously about what is required, one is already thinking in terms with which psychotherapists are familiar.

Many seem to believe that 'learning about religion' is essentially a matter of intellectual maturity, a cognitive grasp of fact and doctrine, philosophical ability, historical understanding of the major or 'higher' religions and so on. From this it seems to follow that only in the sixth form, if then, can we seriously hope to deal with the reasonableness or unreasonableness of particular religions, or to gain any adequate conception of what it is like to believe in them. But, as we have seen, there are certain quite ordinary emotions, common to all human beings even when they are very young, which underlie these complicated metaphysical and doctrinal structures: and any picture of 'understanding religion' which makes it similar to understanding the Nicene creed or Spinoza's metaphysics is a false picture. The metaphysical or doctrinal superstructure is, in one very real sense, unimportant in itself: it is the kind of emotions to which it bears witness that we have to detect and educate.

Granted this, there seems no *a priori* reason to believe that age, I.Q., or intellectual maturity and sophistication are of crucial importance. Characteristics such as insight and self-awareness are to be found amongst younger children as well as in the sixth form: indeed one might argue, rightly or wrongly, that some of these may actually diminish as we become more intellectually sophisticated and psychologically well-defended. In fact we do and should expect young children to understand their own and other people's emotions and outlooks: by getting them to act out their emotions, role-playing, the use of video-tape and other methods of 'showing them to themselves', films, simple literature, games and simulated situations, we believe that it is possible for them to become more 'emotionally educated'. And if emotionally educated, to that (very important) extent educated in religion.

Context

In practice many religious groups, or groups who attach themselves to some other type of ideal or metaphysic, do not educate us very much at all: that is, they do not deliberately use particular methods or contexts to develop the rationality of their adherents. Either the methods or contexts are not used deliberately at all (but just uncritically accepted); or else they are used to indoctrinate or reinforce some particular set of attitudes, beliefs or emotions. What we have first to do is to free ourselves from both of these mistakes. The question is not 'What contexts (church services, meetings, etc.) are somehow in themselves right and proper, or traditional, or correctly reflect and reinforce the beliefs of a particular sect or religion?' but rather 'What contexts will help us to become more reasonable and sane?' This is an open question, and (partly) an empirical one, the answer to which will depend very much on who we are.

The history of religious and metaphysical groups has in general shown them either hostile to this approach or ignorant of it. Characteristically most adults, responding to external social pressures and internal psychological ones, have adopted a religion or an ideal which suits (or appears to suit) their own mental make-up, used those contexts of worship or group activity which fit the religion of the ideal, and been content or anxious for their children to use the same contexts. For example, some people appear to need an external authority to whom they submit, and who will decide moral and other questions for them. The orthodox Roman Catholic church supplies (or used to supply) this need, not only by Papal pronouncements, but also by a type of ritual and hierocratic structure in which the authority is very evident. People with a more egalitarian bias may be members of a nonconformist sect, where more stress is laid on individual conscience and less on obedience: and the services of such sects, as well as their doctrines, reflect this preference. We may trace here a dimension on various points of which we may place certain sects, creeds, ideals and so forth: the authority-freedom dimension. It would of course be grossly oversimplified to put (say) the Roman church and the Communists at one end, and at the other the Quakers; but the point is plain enough.

Now there is a similar dimension, at one end of which stands the notion of reinforcement, and at the other the notion of education or therapy. In many, perhaps most, social contexts we do not learn: we enjoy ourselves, make ourselves feel more secure, get rid of excessive emotions, and feel at one with our neighbours. The purpose (whether conscious or not) of a Nazi rally, a dinner party, a fiesta, and most of the features of religious services is not to improve our emotions by cognitive understanding, but (in various ways) to keep the participants happy – to relieve their guilt, uplift their spirits, give them a sense of social solidarity, inspire them to communal action and so forth. These objectives are of the greatest importance, and we must not decry such contexts simply because they are not educational. Human beings cannot spend all their time learning: and it is not clear that they should even if they could. Everybody needs these contexts, not least children and adolescents. But such contexts, although necessary for education, are not themselves educational contexts. Thus a church service with a fixed pattern of ritual and symbolic acts may help an individual's security, by offering an institutionalized form which fits his mental state: but it will not *teach* him anything. The sermon and the private confessional may tend to be more educative: and the kind of discussion and meditation that takes place in some sects (for example the Quakers) is still more so. Usually, however, the religious contexts are not contexts of learning, but contexts in which (at the least) a certain type of atmosphere is, as it were, expected to sink into and influence the individual of itself. This atmosphere may be encouraged by music, décor, dress, ritual silences, bodily postures and so forth: even in the lowest of the low-church sects the context is not quite that of a seminar or a discussion-group.

Once we get rid of the idea of uncritically accepting particular contexts (which may make neither for security nor for therapy)

H

simply because they are there, or are part of some tradition for which we still have some hankering, it will be seen that we have a far wider choice in practical matters than might have been supposed. Thus the question 'What shall we do about morning assembly?' has to be tackled in an appropriately wide framework. The right questions to ask are: 'Do we want to have the whole school together in one place? Where? When? For what sort of purpose – reinforcement (social solidarity, etc.) or educational? What sort of activities will achieve this purpose?' These questions go far beyond such issues as whether to have hymns or not, or whether to allow other literature besides the Bible to be read.

For learning about religion is not a matter merely of instruction: we also require experience. In trying to educate children in those areas commonly called 'musical appreciation' on 'drama', we are not content merely to *instruct* them. They also *take part in* concerts and plays. So too with religion. Provided we keep our aims clearly in mind, there is an obvious case to be made for having those experiences of religion that may be gained by particular forms of worship. 'Communal acts of worship' in the school may in principle be thus justified: and the experiences which we might gain by taking part in many different types of worship – not only Roman Catholic, Church of England, Methodist, etc. but also Jewish, Mohammedan, Buddhist and so forth – are obviously valuable.

Conclusion

What I have written above can do no more than point to some of the ways along which we can progress. It leaves many questions unanswered. But, to conclude, I should like to emphasize again two points which have been implicit through this book, and without which there would have been no point writing the book at all. The points are simply these: *religion is important, and it is within the scope of reason.* First whatever you may feel about religion – whether you are 'for' it or 'against' it, whether you believe that we ought to worship anything or not, whatever religious faith you may or may not have been brought up in – you cannot escape its importance; for that importance is the importance of human emotions, from which there is no escape (though many of us try to find one). Second, although no one has the right to force (brow-beat, indoctrinate, etc.) you into believing anything or taking any particular attitude, you cannot make up your mind about religion without trying to think about it properly. It is no good just picking the religion that happens to appeal to you, or dismissing the whole thing as silly, or following the fashion, or doing anything else except *think*. Thinking is hard work. To do it properly we need all the help we can get from other people, from books, discussion, different types of experience, and so on. Any fool can follow his fancy or his fantasy: it takes a sensible person to think properly about it. If this book helps at all to show what religion is, and how to start thinking about it, then it will have done its job.

appendix

Awe and its Objects

IN THE main text of Part I, I have tied the notion of religion to the concepts of awe and worship; and I hope there to have shown that this link is a reasonable one, whatever problems may arise about these concepts. Nevertheless, problems *do* arise. In particular, there are a number of important questions which may enter the reader's mind, and which ought to be pursued further (though I cannot even here do them complete justice). I will try to list these questions, and say something about them, by way of amplifying some of the points in Part I.

Causes and 'targets' of awe
One question that may arise is this: are there really any *appropriate objects* of awe, or is awe just something that we (or some of us) feel on odd occasions, sparked off by some unknown cause? I have in mind the kind of distinction we make between ordinary emotions like fear and what seem to be 'object-less' emotions: to the latter we sometimes give special names – we say 'He has a phobia about spiders', or talk of 'free-floating anxiety', meaning that there is nothing for the person to be anxious *about*. If a man is frightened of something dangerous, like elephants or poisonous spiders, this is straightforward and understandable. But men may also be frightened or 'have a phobia' about harmless spiders, or about crossing running water: and this is odd, because (we think) how *can* they really be frightened *about these things* since (as we have just said) there is nothing for them to be frightened about?

In some at least of these cases, it is not just that the man has some obviously false belief about the object of his fear. He may know perfectly well that the spider is harmless and still be frightened – it is not that he thinks it is a dangerous tarantula, and stops being frightened when he learns that it is harmless. He is, as it were, *just frightened*, as one may be 'just depressed' or 'just feel happy' quite irrespective of whether one's life is going well or badly.

Wittgenstein drew a distinction here between the causes of an emotion and what he called its 'target'.[1] It is one thing to be frightened in the presence of spiders, when spiders are around: another thing to be frightened *of* them. The difference is that in the second case a man sees something (spiders) in a certain light: he sees them as dangerous or terrifying: whereas in the first case this need not be so. He need not even know that the spiders are there – it may be their smell, or a half-heard rustling noise as they move, which is the cause of his alarm. In the same way a man may be made happy or gay or joyous by getting drunk: that is the *cause* of his feeling. But he is not happy *at* the drink, so to speak – the drink is not the *target* of his feeling. All feelings have causes: not all have targets.

With the causes of awe I am not here concerned: that is a matter for psychologists. But it seems clear that awe also has targets, at least characteristically. Certainly there are some, perhaps many, cases where a person is seized by a 'nameless dread' – where he has no idea what he is in awe *of*. But there are also plenty of cases where he does know. It is his boss, his queen, his totem-pole, his statue of the Madonna. So at first glance, anyway, 'awe' is not the name of some emotion which is necessarily irrational and 'object-less', as 'phobia' or 'free-floating anxiety' or 'nameless dread'. There is at least the *possibility* – that is, the logical possibility – of awe having appropriate targets, since awe can at least have targets.

Appropriate targets
But this does not get us very far. We have seen that being in awe is not (always) like being drunk and happy, or being depressed – it is not just a feeling that overtakes us, with no target but only a cause. But to show that awe can have targets or objects is not to show that it can have *appropriate* ones. If awe is not like being drunk and happy, it might be like being romantically in love. Romantic love

[1] See references in A. Kenny's *Action, Emotion and Will* (Routledge).

is directed to a target (the beloved); but we often think it to be an inappropriate target, and some might claim that the target is always inappropropriate. Just as it cannot, surely, be anything *about the harmless spiders themselves* that makes the man frightened, so (some might say) it is not anything real about the actual beloved person that produces romantic love – it is, rather, something which he 'sees in her', something which the beloved stands for, or symbolizes, or unconsciously reminds him of.

Thus a psychoanalyst might say (and with some force) that the beloved is not really the target of his romantic love. The feeling is understandable and appropriate, say, for a very young child towards his mother – his mother is immensely important for him, and contains all that he knows of beauty and love and longing – and it is simply that the adult lover sees his beloved as if she were his mother, or as symbolizing his mother in certain respects. In the same way various gods, for religious people, are in fact only symbols of their earlier experiences: it is really their fathers and mothers, or other immensely powerful features of their early life, that they are in awe of. The target of awe only appears to be the totem-pole, the statue of the Madonna, the picture of Jesus (in the mind or on canvas).

There seems to me no doubt at all that this is true of a very great part of religious belief. Believers have, quite plainly, 'made their gods in their own image', and as it were adjusted their picture of god to fit their own childhood feelings. We have seen something in Part II of how social, as well as psychological, changes may alter the believer's picture of the object of his awe. We have to accept that much, perhaps most, of actual religion is of this kind: that is, it is an unconscious attempt on the part of the believer to *create* a fantasy-world of objects which he (already) wants to be in awe of. This process is not normally within the believer's control: it is something which overtakes him, something which he just finds himself doing (as we find ourselves romantically in love, rather than choosing to be in love).

But it does not follow from this that there *can* be no appropriate objects of awe. To take parallels: it may well be that many or most of the things that men in present and past ages have admired, or loved, or thought beautiful, or revered, or felt loyalty towards, were in a sense their own creations or inventions, reflecting their own particular (often neurotic) needs. It was not really the hero, the girl, the song, the monument, the nation *in themselves* – that is, as described by some neutral and unaffected observer – which moved them, but their own transfiguration of these things into something different. And indeed sometimes men have come to see this: a man may come to see that a song he had thought beautiful is in fact rather cheap and sentimental – it was just the sentimental associations which lured him into admiring it. But, as this example itself shows, none of this makes us suppose that there are not genuine or 'real' heroes, lovely girls, beautiful songs, venerable buildings, inspiring causes, etc. Because men make mistakes and deceive themselves, we do not propose to banish admiration, reverence, and so on from human life, as we might wish to banish irrational phobias.

Criteria for appropriateness

But even this is not much. For, granted that there is the bare logical possibility of appropriate awe, what are the criteria of appropriateness? Here we have to distinguish sharply between logical and other points. First, there are points about when we can intelligibly apply the word 'awe' (or other words in other languages). Awe, like all emotions, has characteristic beliefs, symptoms and behaviour which make up the concept. People who feel in awe characteristically believe the object of awe to be, in some very general sense, *impressive* and *overwhelming*: they are characteristically in awe of big, powerful and majestic things. Such people put themselves in what we may call a *receptive* posture towards the object: they do not try to act on it or control it or do things with it, but (perhaps) stand wide-eyed before it, abase themselves before it, look up (literally and metaphorically) towards it. They also say things to it or about it which reflect all this – words which glorify it, sing its praises, declare its impressiveness, and so on. When formalized to some degree, these latter activities are what we mean by worship.

There are, then, logical limits to our application of the word 'awe'. But there are no logical limits to the particular things of which one may be in awe. A man *may* see *any* object or person as impressive, majestic, etc. and show the symptoms and behaviour that go along with this belief. Of course, he has to do this if he, or we, are to call it 'awe'. If a man said 'I am in awe of so-and-so, but I see him as a rather silly little person', we should not understand him. But he may, logically, direct his pattern of words, symptoms and behaviour to any object whatsoever: this is to say only that it would not be contradictory to call his feeling 'awe', whatever the object in question.

But secondly, there is a whole host of empirical questions – that is, questions involving facts about human beings and their societies – which are also relevant. Thus it may be odd or unusual to feel awed by certain numbers or arithmetical truths, as the Pythagoreans were (just as it is odd to make a sexual fetish out of shoes or hair or rubber mackintoshes); or it may be very common to feel awed by powerful 'father-figures', at least in certain societies. Moreover, these objects of awe may be more or less socially desirable. In practical terms, it might be useful for a society's unity and strength of purpose to believe in a certain kind of father-god, and believe that they were his chosen people. Conversely, it might prove very obstructive to the progress of mathematics to believe (as the Pythagoreans also believed) that certain numbers were 'unspeakable', and should be hushed up, rather as if they were like malevolent demons.

In considering what criteria might be appropriate, one can of course make use of the kind of 'external' considerations we have just mentioned. Just as it might be *useful* (I do not say it actually is) for children to believe that there is a god who always knows what they are doing, or for warriors to believe that their enemies are inspired by the devil, so it might be useful (comforting, morally beneficial, socially necessary) to be in awe of and worship various things. It may also be true, as some psychologists (notably Jung) might hold, that we cannot escape from being in awe of *something*: that awe is an inevitable human emotion: and that the only question is of what object to attach it to. These 'external' criteria are far from unimportant; but there is something ignoble and (more important) impermanent about them. We may find other ways of fulfilling the same social or psychological functions; and then there will be perhaps no place left for awe.

We need, therefore, 'internal' criteria. The question is, not what is it useful or advantageous to be in awe of, but what is really awesome. We could still (I suppose) try to maintain that, to reasonable grown-ups of the kind that we ought to be, nothing is 'really awesome' or ought to appear awesome. We are no longer children: nothing ought now to seem to us overwhelmingly impressive, majestic, etc., and we ought not to feel humble or totally 'receptive' (as I have called it) in the face of anything. In much the same way we could, perhaps, try to maintain that nothing is 'really disgusting' – a feeling of disgust is something we ought to grow out of: and if people are still disgusted by things, this only shows that they have not grown out of their early childhood. But this seems to me much like the mistake we looked at earlier. There may be very obvious *bad* reasons for finding things awesome – our own child-like dependence on adults, our helplessness as children, and so on: but it does not follow that there are not also *good* reasons.

If there are such good reasons, we need to remember that they must be 'internal' ones. To have certain feelings (of which awe may be one) may be defended on all sorts of grounds. It may be socially useful; it may remind us of our own mortality, our liability as human beings to change and chance; it may lead us towards a greater understanding of 'the human condition'; it may prevent us from having other less desirable feelings; and so on. But these are external or extrinsic reasons – to use them would be rather like saying that one ought to admire Beethoven and Michelangelo because it was in some way *good for one* to do so, rather than because the actual works of art are admirable.

What is awesome, and why worship it?

So far as the question 'What is (really) awesome?' is concerned, I want to stress that the question itself is extremely dangerous – though there are right and wrong answers to it. It is dangerous, or perhaps pointless, in much the same way as a beginner in the arts might find it dangerous or pointless to ask and have answered the question 'Which are the greatest works of art?' Of course we *can* answer it: we can say things like 'Well, Shakespeare rather than Agatha Christie, Beethoven rather than most pop music', and so

on. But, first, we may be wrong – and we are much more likely to
be wrong about awe than about aesthetic admiration; and second,
even if we are right it does not greatly help the inquirer, since *he
has to come to see things for himself*. It is not like asking for the
right answer to a sum and getting it. He has to explore the world
and his own emotional investments in the world: no one can do
this for him (though others can help him do it): and no one can
give him 'the answer'. 'Answers' are, in practice, either misleading
or empty.

But perhaps, if pressed, we can at least say something like this:
Most sophisticated people nowadays (including people who still
call themselves Christians, or adhere officially to some other religious faith) seem to realize that many of the gods, or pictures of
gods, that we have worshipped in the past are mostly our own
projections and fantasies. No simple-minded picture of some
super-being or beings 'out there', 'in the sky', will do any more. No
'supernatural' or magical entities exist, or could exist, to do our
work for us. We are, in a sense, on our own. Nevertheless, we live
in a world which contains many marvellous, impressive and
perhaps awesome things. Towards some of these things we cannot
justifiably always adopt an attitude of superiority and control; for,
as human beings, these things always in some sense stand above
and beyond us, and are outside our power.

These forces appear very often in religious and other literature,
and in our daily lives. We may represent them in a pedestrian way
by words like 'love', 'reason', 'nature', 'art', 'humanity', and so
on; but their force and impressiveness (for anyone who has eyes to
see) can only be brought out during the course of life, or in great
works of literature and art. It is one thing to say 'Yes, certainly,
love is very important' or 'Of course, one must be reasonable' or
'Naturally, there are some very good pieces of music': quite
another thing to see that love and reason and art are not just
useful, or nice, or necessary, or 'life-enhancing', or advantageous,
but *overwhelmingly important*. (Even 'important' does not catch
the right tone.) Before them we must, sometimes, feel humble,
small, receptive, child-like: 'must', because this attitude is appropriate to these objects, and anyone who did not or could not
sometimes feel this would have underestimated them. It is not at

all a question of appreciating or domesticating them, but of feeling and acknowledging their force.

Anyone who acknowledges their force (or the force of whatever other things in the world he may take as truly awesome – I make no claims for my particular list) will want to worship: that is, to acknowledge their 'worth' in some more or less formal or institutionalized way. Worship is simply the institutionalization of awe. In worship we *celebrate* the object of awe, in the sense that we may (more weakly) celebrate Shakespeare's centenary or Lenin's death. Naturally we do this by way of symbols, rituals and other forms: all this is quite familiar both to religious and non-religious people. We may, perhaps, even want to personify these awesome forces, much as the Greek tragedians did in their plays, or (again more weakly) as we personify 'the Spirit of France', or 'the Unknown Warrior'. To worship something is simply to endorse and formalize a feeling of awe which we take to be appropriate, and wish to keep alive.

A good deal of this is bound to sound unreal, because we are accustomed to a long history of humanity in which awe and religious worship have simply been *accepted* as rightly directly towards certain gods, and formalized in certain traditions and institutions. The idea of *inventing* or *discovering* our own more appropriate objects of worship, of building our own religion, inevitably seems strange; and of course such discovery is an enormous task, not something that some new sect of 'believers' can quickly run up, like a prefabricated bungalow. It will be a long time before we are in a position to establish a religion based on adequate psychological insight, rather than on a hotch-potch of fears and fantasies; and we shall never establish it at all if we either cling too loyally to existing religions, or (a greater temptation for our society) refuse to acknowledge the many deep insights and symbols which existing religions, for all their deficiencies, still keep alive. But the task seems a necessary one.

Short Reading List

For PART I (these are philosophical works, in accordance with the subject-matter of Part I)

John Wilson, *Education in Religion and the Emotions* (Heinemann)

L. Wittgenstein, *Lectures and Conversations* (Blackwell)

Basil Mitchell (ed.), *Oxford Readings in the Philosophy of Religion* (O.U.P.)

A. Flew and A. C. MacIntyre (eds.), *New Essays in Philosophical Theology* (S.C.M. Press)

Karl Britton, *Philosophy and the Meaning of Life* (C.U.P.)

For PART II

Ninian Smart, *The Religious Experience of Mankind* (Collins)

S. Freud, *Totem and Taboo* and *The Future of an Illusion* (various editions)

J. C. Flugel, *Man, Morals and Society* (Penguin)

W. Lessa and E. Vogt (eds.), *Reader in Comparative Religion* (New York)

Paul Radin, *Primitive Religion, its Nature and Origin* (New York)

R. C. Zaehner (ed.), *The Concise Encyclopaedia of Living Faiths* (London)

Index

returned on or before
below